Confessions of a Jaguar Owner

A Practical, Ethical, and Metaphysical Guide

Michael Witbeck

Copyright © 2014 Michael Witbeck
The Driveway Press
All rights reserved.

ISBN-13: 978-0615944371
ISBN-10: 061594437X

Cover Design by Nadine Mack

CONTENTS

	Introduction	Pg 5
1	Why You're Glad You Don't Own My Car	Pg 10
2	A Short History of Jaguar Cars	Pg 28
3	Ambushed by a Jaguar	Pg 38
4	The J Gate	Pg 48
5	The License Plate Problem	Pg 54
6	Speed	Pg 65
7	Approval	Pg 85
8	Destinations	Pg 98
9	Driving Properly	Pg 115
10	Relationships: The Jaguar Effect	Pg 123
11	Frequently Asked Questions	Pg 134
12	Buying a Jaguar	Pg 144
	Photo Credits	Pg 157
	About the Author	Pg 158

La vitesse n'est ni un signe, ni une preuve, ni une provocation, ni un défi, mais un élan de bonheur.

-Françoise Sagan

Just wished I'd studied harder, man I could afford a REAL car, like a JAGUAR!

-The Urban Dictionary

Introduction: Mostly True Confessions

Hello. My name is Michael and I own a Jaguar. I wasn't always like this. I used to own sensible cars. I owned a Plymouth Valiant; I owned a Nissan pickup with a fiberglass canopy. I even spent a number of years using only public transportation. Now that's sensible. Even now I have three friends who drive Priuses. But somehow my life has spiraled out of control. Now, not only do I not drive a Prius, I also refuse to accept that the plural of Prius is 'Prii' or 'Priora'. I've gone rogue.

I know that I have to take responsibility for my problem. It didn't just happen; I bought my Jaguar with my own money, hard-earned and never very abundant. My excuse could be that the decision to purchase the car was related to degenerative brain damage or some kind of trauma, but that's not it, at least not entirely. The seeds of my problem were always there. When I was sixteen, I bought a Triumph TR3. Fortunately, I was young and strong and I overcame that moment of weakness after only a year or so. By the time I was twenty-seven I had owned three more cars, all sensible: a Pontiac, a Valiant, and a Pinto. And when I lost the Pinto in a divorce, I rode a bicycle for a year. Because I was good. And also because I was poor. It's true that I hit a rough patch and bought a broken down TR4 at some point. But I didn't keep it long. I rose from that experience even stronger than before. I sold the TR4, moved to a succession of big cities (Tokyo and Barcelona) and rode public transport for five full years. Yes, I admit there were a few car rentals now and then...and that thing with the scooter...but basically I was good. I was so good in fact that after five years of buses and trains, I put in another year commuting to work by bicycle.

How in the world, then, did I end up with a Jaguar? It didn't happen overnight. In the spirit of full disclosure, here's a complete and reasonably honest list of the cars that I have owned. The number in parentheses is the age of the car in years when I acquired it. Asterisks indicate partial ownership.

    1961 Triumph TR3A (7)
    1959 Pontiac Starfire (10)
    1964 Plymouth Valiant (8)
    1977 Ford Pinto (0)
    1964 Triumph TR4 (15)
    1969 Austin-Healey Sprite (17)
    1982 Toyota Land Cruiser (5)
    1986 Nissan King Cab (5)
    1992 Mazda Miata (1)
    2001 Ford Escape (0)*
    2004 Nissan 350Z (0)
    2009 Mercury Mariner Hybrid (0)*
    2004 Jaguar XKR (8)
    2012 Mazda 3 (2)*

In 1985 I was riding a bicycle. In 1986 I bought a 17-year-old Austin-Healey Sprite, fun in its way, but also some painful memories there; let's not dredge them up. When I finally got rid of the Sprite, I swore I'd never have another British car. After that I had a Toyota Land Cruiser. No bad memories there, it was a joy, the perfect car for Yemen, which was where I was living at the time. There weren't any Jaguars in Yemen back then and considering the state of the road system, a Jag was about the last car you'd have wanted even if you could have found one. For a person with a Land Cruiser, though, Yemen was a fantastic place. I left Yemen in 1990, just a few months before the beginning of nasty civil war that I never really understood. I had a sensible car and picked a sensible time to leave the area. As I was preparing to leave I sold the Land Cruiser. It would have been insane--so I thought--to try and ship it back to the U.S. Such a sensible guy. Now, though, I'd give an awful lot to have it around. Hmm.

Anyway, there is no question that the Land Cruiser was a practical and sensible vehicle, admirably suited to the local environment. And so were the cars that followed: the pickup, the Miata, the Escape and the Z. There are some people who might object to calling a Miata practical. And it's true that for a family of five who want to get by with only one car, a Miata might be pretty foolish. But back in the nineties, Miatas were cheap to buy, cheap to operate and never broke down. They made driving fun and were perfectly adequate for 95% of the things that a childless person might want to do with a car. Okay, that's fine, someone might be saying at this point, but what about the 350Z? I suppose you're going to say that it was just like the Miata, just with a little bigger trunk and a little nicer cabin? Exactly, and now moving right along, we come to the Mariner Hybrid. Of course this was also sensible; it was a hybrid. It got great mileage! It's true that it was a highly optioned model and my that wife and I had to spend almost all our savings to get it and that we made the purchase right in the midst of a national financial meltdown, but those were just cracks in the facade of good sense. I like to think that the basic mental structure was still sound. So it is only when we come to the Jaguar that things seem to go haywire.

I'll be talking more about how and why this lapse occurred in some of the following chapters, but here are the basics, the gritty details. I found myself becoming restless, filled with a low-grade but persistent longing to change cars. I realized the concept of owning a Jaguar had burrowed its way into my brain. I looked and looked, and then I pounced, making the purchase over the internet, dealing with a very sincere fellow down in California. More about him later also. The upshot was that I agreed to hand over some cash and a 350Z and he was going to give me this Jaguar thing. A pleasant young assistant of his drove it up to Oregon and arrived at my house at about ten in the morning. His girlfriend was with him. We talked for a while and signed some papers. Then he drove away in my 350Z. So there I was, sans Z, sans cash. I was standing in my driveway, looking at a Jaguar, wondering what to think. Well, well, well. Did you ever hear the joke about the three holes? Well. Well. Well.

In part, this book is an attempt to explain how and why that moment occurred and what I have done to try and deal with it. I hope it will be of some assistance, or at least amusement, to anyone who has had a similar aberration. Don't expect me to be revealing any secrets or useful hints related to Jaguar maintenance and repair because I don't know any. Minor confession #1: I don't know even know where the oil filter is on my Jaguar. Apparently it is hidden behind a cover. Fine. Let someone else find it. Self-reliance may be generally a good thing, but I'm not sure that owners of modern Jaguars should be puttering around trying to fix their cars by themselves. On the other hand, some of the mechanical and electronic systems in the Jaguar are interesting and worth trying to understand, so I'll get into them at times. But the real challenges of Jaguar ownership lie elsewhere, not so much mechanical as philosophical, possibly spiritual. First of all, you have to admit you have a problem...

Neither is this a guide to how to drive really fast and have a wild exciting life. For one thing--and this is minor confession #2--I'm a dilettante when it comes to driving fast. True speed racers will be able to see that just by looking at the list of cars I've owned. One giveaway is that so many of my cars have been convertibles. Serious people drive coupes because coupes are stiffer, lighter and faster. My vehicle history puts me somewhere on the non-serious side of things in terms of speed. Of course, even us non-serious drivers are aware of the concept of speed, or 'pace' as we say in Jaguarland, so I will have to touch on that too, just a little.

So this book will discuss the notion of speed--heck, there's a whole chapter on the topic--but it will not urge you to go out and rent track time nor will it contain any hints about how to

Introduction

shave seconds and tenths of seconds off your laps because, frankly, shaving off those seconds is hard work and most Jaguars were never set up to be racing cars anyway. So what are they set up for? What am I doing with one? The jury is still out on whether I even like this Jag. My wife misses the 350Z. Why would that be so? What is it that we like or don't like about our cars and how they carry us around? How much of a car's identity is real and how much is marketing hype combined with our own romantic imaginations? Both my Jaguar and my old Nissan were new in 2004. At that time the Jaguar was almost three times as expensive as the Nissan. Was it three times as much car? Is that even possible? Or is it all just a scam? Eight years later, both cars had depreciated a good deal, but the used Jag was still two times as expensive as the used Nissan. Did it look twice as good? Did it go twice as fast? Was it likely to last twice as long? Was it twice as much of pleasure to drive? Or was just a huge mistake on my part? I didn't really know much going in. This book is about what I found out.

Chapter 1: Why You're Glad You Don't Own My Car

My Jaguar is a 2004. It's an XKR, a supercharged version of the XK8, a model first produced in 1996. The Jaguar XK8 was considered a success back when it first arrived. People raved about its good looks, its high tech suspension and its beautiful interior. Reviewers also praised its handling and were pleased with the engine, a light and powerful V-8. The engine was a brand new design, only the fourth completely new engine in Jaguar history, replacing the wonderful but complex and aging Jaguar V-12. Contemporary reviewers made comparisons to the famous Jaguars of the past--the XK8 was said to be a worthy successor to the famous XK120 of the fifties and the even more famous E-Type of the sixties.

I'll talk more about the XK 120 and the E-Type in the next chapter; here, I'll just mention that while they both fit the classic definition of a sports car--and perhaps even helped create that definition--the 1996 XK8 did not. The new car wasn't overly large, but it felt large--large and comfortable. Sports cars feel small and agile, and comfortable is not the most common description. In terms of the physical layout, the new XK8 had four seats, but a true sports car can only have two. It's true that the XK8's rear seats were useless for sitting on since they had no legroom whatever, but they still added considerable weight and changed the look and feel of the car.

The new car would better be categorized as a grand touring car. Grand tourers are supposed to be fast and agile, but also elegant-looking and comfortable. They are always expensive. The distinction between an expensive sports car and a grand touring car can get blurry, as in the case of certain Ferraris, but the difference is still useful. From Germany, Porsches 911s, Porsche Boxsters, and BMW Z-4s are all clearly sports cars while other BMW's and certain Mercedes Benz's lean toward the grand tourers, even in the case of some Mercedes models that only have two seats. Among U.S. carmakers, there is one sports car, the Corvette, and one or two sports sedans with grand touring tendencies. Otherwise, Americans are busy with their pickup trucks, their SUVs and their muscle cars. From Japan, the Mazda Miata, the Honda S2000, and the Nissan 350Z are all sports cars, while Acura, Lexus and Infiniti compete in the grand touring and sports sedans markets.

My 2004 Jaguar XKR is not so different from that original 1996 XK8: the same body and layout, very similar suspension, very similar interior. It's a heavy car, weighing just over 4000 pounds, and it feels like it. So it's definitely in the grand touring family as opposed to the sports car family. There are, however, two differences between a regular XK8 and my car, an XKR. One difference is the supercharger, which means that the engine produces a lot more power. Another difference is that my XKR has oversize wheels and low profile tires. That makes the handling sharper (maybe) and takes away a bit of comfort (definitely). These two things nudge the car a bit closer to sports car territory, though they don't quite get it there.

Now I don't want to go on and on about categories, but I'm going to be making some comparisons in this chapter and I want to at least lean in the direction of comparing apples to apples. To really know what you're getting into if you buy a Jaguar--or what you have already gotten yourself into if you just acquired one--you need to identify the car's general category and it then look at its peer group. As far as categories go, my car is a mishmash of a grand tourer, a wannabe sports car and a fine art collectible along the lines of a Steiff bear, which is one of the reasons why you're glad you don't own it.

Your Jaguar, though, might be more clearly defined. The XK120/40/50, the E-Type, and the F-Type are all sports cars. The XJ cars--in their many iterations--are luxury grand tourers. The S-Type and XF are luxury sport sedans, or 'executive cars' in Britspeak.

But let's get back to our particular test case--the XKR. As I try to explain to you why you should be glad you don't own my car, I'm going to mention a number of the car's specific characteristics, but many of these characteristics are a matter of personal preferences. How do I know what your preferences are? You might be weird. So I'll save those for later. First I need some data, something that will appeal to reason. Fortunately, there is something objective that we can use here to compare the XKR to other cars, something with numbers, those rational and logical things. And that, of course, is price, specifically the used car price. It's pretty clear that the price of any used car is directly equivalent to its general desirability. So what if we take a group of cars that are roughly similar in category and that were all similarly priced when they were new and see how they fare as used cars when they are eight or nine years old, that being the age today of my Jaguar, the car you're glad you don't own. The idea here is that within this group the better cars will be those which have held value best.

To begin, let's pick the peer group. Our first contender will be the 2004 Porsche 911 Carrera 4 Cabriolet. This was a convertible Porsche and had a bit of a luxury tinge to it. It's firmly in the sports car category, but has been nudged a little toward grand touring territory. When they were new in 2004, they cost anywhere from $83,000 to $98,000, depending on options. As we mentioned in the Introduction, convertibles are a bit frivolous in the car world. And in the Porsche world in 2004 there were actually two convertibles, the aforementioned Carrera 4 Cabriolet, and the Carrera Turbo Cabriolet, which was meaner, faster and even more expensive, i.e., more serious. Therefore we must conclude that Carrera 4 Cabriolets are cars that appealed to the non-serious Porsche purchaser. Hmm. After a moment's quiet consideration of that seemingly self-contradictory concept, let's push on.

Our second contender is the 2004 Mercedes SL500. This was a hardtop convertible, which in this case means a rigid metal retractable top, a remarkable mechanism that provided the best of both worlds but which took up an awful lot of trunk space. It had a bit less power than the Porsche, but more luxury. Handling was super refined and electronic gizmos abounded. It's a grand touring car encroaching on sports car territory. The price in 2004 was from $88,500 to around $100,000. (Mercedes also made faster and more expensive versions of the SL500--the SL500 AMG and the SL600; but as with the Porsche Turbo mentioned above, their price points put them beyond the parameters of this comparison.)

Third comes the Maserati Cambiocorsa. Modern Maserati autos are the definitive grand touring machines: stylish, powerful, and comfortable. These days they are produced under the aegis of Ferrari. They may not aspire to the pure racing performance of their siblings, but they do aspire to be fast and joyous in the real world. The 4.2 liter V-8 in the 2004 Spyder shares its basic design with a Ferrari motor. It offers nearly the same power as the XKR without the need for supercharging. And because the Spyder is lighter than the Jag, the Maserati is considerably faster, with a claimed 0-60 time of just 4.8 seconds. Contemporary reviewers praised the engine to the skies, but some had issues with the rather budget level navigation and stereo systems and with the convertible top. Prices ranged from $94,000 to $100,000.

And fourth comes our Jaguar XKR. As we have seen, this is another grand tourer with some sports car pretensions. It was faster and more powerful than the Mercedes and had its own suite of electronic aids, superior to the Maserati if not quite equal to the Merc. Its convertible top, though solid and reliable, was the most primitive of the group. Prices ranged from $85,000 to $94,000.

As can be seen on the following pages, all these cars look pretty good and you probably wouldn't be ashamed to own any of them. In fact, in 2004, they were the latest and shiniest thing. They were all pretty expensive back then too; you had to be

Confessions of a Jaguar Owner

Red Porsche Carrera convertible, photographed by Norbert Aepli at the Geneva Auto Show. This is actually a 2005, but in appearance it's not so different from the 2004. The wheels suggest speed, but in a somewhat businesslike way. The spectators wear suits.

New blue-gray Maserati convertible photographed at the Genena Auto Show by Semnoz, March 12, 2004. Spectators must wear suits and pretend not to be interested. The wheels appear to be from a Denali.

Why You're Glad You Don't Own My Car

Mercedes Benz SL500 photographed in 2004 by Bollar. The wheels are similar to the Porsche's but more restrained. Sorry, no spectators are allowed in the Mercedes area.

Jaguar XKR convertible photographed at a car show in Sweden by Magnus Bäck. Nice color on this car--if you like black. The optional 20-inch wheels are pretty, but too showy--special, but not as special as the ones on my car! The spectators wear sweaters and eat Swedish tacos or something.

pretty well fixed to even think about one. But what was the story nine years later? The table below shows how the cars stack up in terms of retained value after nine years. For each car I have listed first the manufacturer's suggested retail price for a moderately optioned car when it was new. To account for inflation, I've expressed the 2004 suggested retail prices in terms of 2013 dollars. In the third column I've listed an average 2013 asking price for each car. In working up the averages I have excluded super low mileage collector cars and also all non-running or damaged cars. The last column shows the percentage of value retained. Just for fun, I've added a Toyota Camry family sedan to the mix, a top of the line V-6 XLE.

2004 cars	2004 price (in 2013 $)	Used price in 2013	Retained value
Camry	$31,435	$13,250	42%
Porsche	$112,000	$37,500	33%
Maserati	$119,600	$25,000	21%
Mercedes	$116,650	$24,500	21%
Jaguar	$110,750	$21,500	19%

So, are there any 2004 Camry owners out there? If so, you win. In 2013 your car was still worth close to half of what you paid for it. Porsche Cabriolet buyers, serious or not, you're looking pretty smart too, with your 33% retained value. Mercedes SL500 buyers, you are losers, but you probably don't care. If you do care, you can take some comfort from the fact that at least you didn't buy a Jaguar XKR. As for you Maserati Cambiocorsa drivers--and there aren't that many of you out there--I have to first say that my estimate of used Maserati prices is kind of shaky.

As I was researching this, I found quite a number of 2002 to 2005 Cambiocorsas offered for sale, but none met my 60,000 mile qualification. There were a couple in the 50,000 mile range, but the vast majority were in the teens, twenties or thirties. In general, Cambiocorsa people just don't drive much. Prices are strong for cars with up to 25,000 or so miles, but they kind of drop off a cliff somewhere in the thirties. So my price estimate of $25,000 has to be taken with a large grain of salt.

No question about the Jaguar, though; it's last. I told you you're glad you don't own one and now the marketplace has confirmed it. Perhaps, however, a stray reader here or there might not be convinced, might not yet be truly glad that she does not own this car. This rapid depreciation might actually be good news, such a reader might suddenly interject, because if for whatever reason you do want a 2004 Jaguar XKR in 2013 or whenever, it's has now become affordable. It's within reach. It's a bargain. No, no, no, I must reply. That just makes it worse! That's what makes it tempting. You have to keep in mind that you don't really want this car, at least not this particular one.

There are some special things not to like about this car. In the first place it's not just an XKR, it's an XKR Portfolio Edition. What's that, you might well ask. Yes, you well might. Basically, it's a scam. Only two hundred Portfolio edition cars were made, one hundred in Jupiter Red and one hundred in Coronado Blue. The idea of these special edition cars was to try and make a car that was instantly collectible and extra expensive. It's a marketing thing and in this particular case the only really special thing was the price. Portfolio XKR's were priced $9,000 higher than regular XKRs. And what did one get for that? A special paint color, special matching colored leather interior, and different, extra special wheels. That's it. Were these differences worth $9,000 in 2004? Well that depends; there's no accounting for taste. I'm almost certain I wouldn't have thought so if I had been buying a new XKR in 2004. But I've never had either $85,000 or $94,000 to spend on a car, so what do I know?

Let me hasten to explain how I ended up with this scam car. My problem was color. There were no cars anywhere near me, so I had to do my searching on the internet. The vast majority of the cars I found for sale were black or silver. Dullsville. Black is a fine color on a limo or a hearse but ridiculous on a sports car. In 2004 black was definitely "in" or at least someone thought it was. Jaguar actually offered two different shades of black that year! They also did a lot of silver, but silver is just a fancy way of painting something gray, which I thought was just a light shade of black. Fool that I was. It turns out that gray Jaguars can be quite beautiful, but I didn't understand that until very recently when I finally saw one in person. Very nice. Très élégant. And gray matches the landscape around here. But never mind. Gray wasn't for me.

I might have tolerated white, but white seems to have been a rare color choice in that era and I couldn't find one in my target zone of price, age, mileage and location. I would have taken blue in an instant, but again, no luck. I found a California car in a nice, somewhat subdued shade of red, Jupiter Red, used only on the Portfolio Edition. I was tired of searching, too impatient to wait around and hope for something better. So I'm stuck with this rare edition car, a point that came to the fore after just a few months of ownership when I had to face up to my damaged wheels.

The car had some wheel damage when I bought it, mostly cosmetic, but something I definitely wanted to fix--someday. Then, just a few months in, I drove too close to a curb and scratched up another wheel, scrunching it badly. Sigh. Now I had to really deal with it. Careful scrutiny made me realize that I actually had three 'damaged' or should I say 'less than perfect' wheels and only one good one. The left front wheel was in near perfect condition. Fine. The right front was the one I had really messed up on an otherwise thoroughly satisfactory trip to the Oregon coast. This was definitely not good. The left rear had a more serious flaw that the dealer had been smart enough to point out to me when I bought the car. Not good, but something you could almost live with, almost but not quite. The right rear wheel was pretty good, though it had a small flaw that I had hitherto overlooked. So, what to do?

Did I mention that these are not the normal XK8/XK18-inch wheels, and not even the normally optional 19 or 20-inch wheels? Oh no, these are different. They are 20-inch split rim BBS wheels, code named 'Detroit' for some reason, that only came on the Portfolio edition XKRs. We can't just order some new ones from Tire Rack; they're not available.

So, what can one do? I saw two options. One would be to

purchase four replacement wheels, all shiny and new, not real BBS Detroits, but quite reasonably priced and similar enough so that no normal sane passerby would ever notice or care. This would be expensive, say $1200 or so, but you might be able to sell at least two of the old BBS wheels on eBay, recouping some of your cost. That would be a lot of trouble, but if all went well the net cost would be less than $1000--possibly a lot less, depending on how much one could get for the old wheels. And the car would look great. Alternatively, one could try to get the BBS wheels repaired. This option would be considerably more expensive. What? Fixing two old wheels would be more expensive that buying four new ones? Oh yes. So why would you do that? Well, it would maintain the car's original condition, hence in theory making it more desirable as a collectible. The next buyer might not know or care about BBS, in which case spending so much money to fix them would be cash down the drain. But the next buyer also might be someone who, for whatever reason, really wants the original BBS wheels to be there. You never know about people. Some of them are nuts.

Speaking of which, I have chosen to go the BBS route and as of this writing I am still in the midst of that process, having paid a great deal of money to get the worst wheel repaired and currently saving up to do the next worst wheel next winter. BBS wheels are a minor automotive legend and I want them, just as I like having seats by Recaro and brakes by Brembo. These famous names soothe the ego, in a sort of a sick kind of way, especially if you've heard about them for a long time but never had them before on your very own car.

And then there's the matter of tires. When I took possession of my Jaguar the rear tires were worn out and the front tires, though newish, were an obscure Asian brand called Nexen. The car was crying out for a set of four new tires, preferably the original equipment tires, Pirelli P-Zeros. That would be really cool. It would also cost over $1500. Is there a cheaper option? How about a really cheap option? Like if you ran into someone who had two used but almost new Nexens in exactly the size that fit the rear wheels and you bought them for $100 each.

Okay, that was fortuitous, that was lucky. But, we realize with a sigh, now we'll never know what the car would have felt like with really good tires.

So, are you convinced yet about the XKR? In terms of overall value, the marketplace has spoken and the answer is no. In the critical automotive matter of making contact with the road, the wheels are fragile and very expensive to repair and the cost of replacement OEM tires is ridiculous. That's all very well, another reader might say--a normal, sane reader, one in possession of all his faculties--but what about fun? It must be really fun to drive. Well...yeah...maybe. In fact I am starting to think that it is pretty fun to drive and I'll be trying to explain that in some of the later chapters. But first, I have a few things to say about why it isn't that much fun to drive.

The Jaguar is smooth and sophisticated, but that's not the same thing as fun. It goes back to something at the beginning of this chapter, the difference between a sports car and a grand touring car. Sports cars are meant to be instantly responsive to driver inputs and to provide immediate useful feedback about the resulting conditions. This is summed up nicely by the Miata's design credo: *jinba ittai*, horse and rider as one. This gets into a sort of mystical realm beyond the innocent concept of mere fun, but it represents one ideal of driving enjoyment, an ideal toward which all sports cars aspire. As we shall see later on, grand touring cars aspire to a somewhat different ideal. Another factor that weighs on the fun quotient is technology, specifically the electronic systems that are used in modern cars to enhance safety, but which have the added effect of filing off the edges of the driving experience.

Lets start with something called active suspension, which has been available on some cars since the nineties. There are different sorts. The Jaguar system is called, cutely enough, CATS, computer active technology suspension. The purpose of such systems is to keep the tires perpendicular to and in firm contact with the road at all times, no matter what the car may be doing. Keeping tires perpendicular and in contact with the road is not an issue when you're just driving along in a straight line, but if you're braking, accelerating, or turning--and especially if you're doing two of those things at the same time-- the laws of physics tend to push things out of whack. Active suspension systems are able to push back and counteract this when necessary. They use sensors to monitor what's going on in terms of a car rocking or tipping to one side (roll) or rocking forward or back (pitch). They then make physical adjustments to the suspension to cancel these motions. The CATS system adds weight and is expensive to fix when it breaks, but it does sort of work miracles. Many cars now have some kind of active or semi-active suspension system.

Another electronic system on the Jaguar (and its competitors) is called DSC, dynamic stability control. It also uses sensors at all four wheels, this time monitoring whether any of the wheels are slipping at all. If the DSC control module gets word that a wheel is slipping, it takes immediate steps to stop it. It has the ability to apply the brakes to individual wheels if it thinks this will help or to cut power to either or both of the drive wheels if that seems indicated. You may wonder if I have ever experienced this system in action. I wonder too! Actually, I think yes, yes I have, but the sensation is subtle. In fact, the point of a sophisticated DSC system is that it happens so fast that your wheel spin problem is corrected even before you become aware of it. Well, that's pretty impressive, but you can see where this is leading. It's leading toward cars that always behave themselves and that are always composed, even if the driver doesn't always behave and isn't always composed. The laws of physics still apply, but now the driver doesn't notice them so much. How much fun can you get from something that you don't notice?

There's a place in my neighborhood where I often make a right hand turn onto a street that climbs up a fairly steep slope. Naturally I tend to get on the gas a bit about halfway through this turn so as to get up the hill in a sprightly manner. Now let's say I'm doing this in the autumn and it's raining. The road is covered with slippery wet maple leaves. If I get on the gas too much, the rear tires slip on the leaves and start spinning, losing all traction. That means they're not making me go forward anymore, but that's not the worst thing. The real problem is

Best not to go too fast up this hill, because there are houses up there. Small herds of humans have been spotted in the area.

So I like to turn right up this hill. But it's funny how grip can suddenly disappear, especially if these leaves get wet. Let's keep the traction control on.

that since I'm turning sharply to the right, centrifugal forces are pushing me toward the ditch to my left instead of up the hill. I was counting on my tires to grip the road and counteract that. Well, my front tires are still gripping a little, but the rears are not. This means that the rear of the car is swinging wide to the left, the car is moving sideways instead of forward, and the ditch is becoming a real possibility. The solution to the problem is to get off the gas a little and hope that the rear wheels manage to get their grip back. Now of course I can do that myself, but a traction control system can do it faster and better. It can sense rear wheel spin and loss of traction faster than I can and it's also quicker than I am to cut off the power to the wheel. Now back in my Nissan days there were a number of times when I put in a little too much power on this slippery turn. There would be a small loss of grip before the traction control system cut the power resulting in a sudden noticeable drop in speed, at which point the grip came back and the power resumed. It made for a real speed hiccup and my progress up the hill was no longer quite so sprightly, but neither did I come anywhere near the ditch.

On many cars, including the Z, traction control can be turned off. And if you do that, you can have a little more fun. One thing you probably shouldn't do, though, is to spend some time playing around with traction control off and then forget to turn it back on, especially if you're planning make a hard right turn up a hill on some wet maple leaves. That would be dumb.

So, to recap, the Z had traction control, which meant that as soon as it sensed that one of the rear wheels was losing traction, it cut power until traction returned. Fine. It worked, but it was fairly intrusive and it also intervened sometimes when it wasn't wanted or needed, like quite often when I was driving downhill on a straight road and had just shifted into fourth gear. (That was ridiculous; I hope Nissan has fixed it by now.) The Jaguar has dynamic stability control, which can both cut power and brake individual wheels. It's another step forward in making cars safer to drive. So far at least, I have noticed it less.

But there we are again. If you don't notice it, how much fun is it? Maybe some of us want to notice stuff. Maybe that's why we're driving in the first place. And maybe we don't want the car to make decisions for us either. Some drivers really, really like manual transmissions. Presumably they like being in control of the shift point; they like being directly involved in the change of gear ratios; and if they're like me, they also like the experience of feeling and hearing the engine revving up into its power band at higher and higher rpms, and then pausing and falling back to lower rpms in the new gear. Acceleration falters at this point, stopping entirely during the pause to shift, and then resuming with less oomph than it had at its peak, but then gradually building back up to that peak, only to pause once again during the shift to the next higher gear. These 'noticeable' things, the change in sound from rumble to roar to shriek and the accompanying changes in one's sense of acceleration, result directly from the rising and falling rpm.

    I say that it starts with a rumble, but that's only in a certain kind of car; most cars start from a quiet little swishing sound at idle speed, which is somewhere around 600 engine revolutions per minute. Six hundred revolutions a minute is slow for an engine, but it's still 10 per second. And what with valves and pistons and all, there's a lot going on in even one revolution. As I said, some engines swish at that speed, but others are so smooth as to be almost eerily silent, which suggests that humans have gotten pretty good at building them. Toyota Camry owners, are you there? A lot of engineering effort goes into making cars quiet because many drivers place a high value on it. They want their cars to be as silent as possible even when the engine is spinning at 3,000 revolutions per minute and the car itself is hurtling along at freeway speeds.

    But that's not everybody's idea of fun. Some drivers want their cars to make noise. They want their cars to rumble at idle, to make some kind of roaring sound at speed, and maybe even howl as they approach their highest revs. Carmakers design cars for these people also. Sports car makers give a lot of attention to exhaust tuning, which is basically a matter of how to make the car sound exciting without exceeding the noise laws. So what if an engine designed for a sporty car turns out to be extremely powerful, wonderful in almost all ways, but not very noisy? BMW faced that problem recently with their high performance M5 sedan. Their new engine was more efficient than the old one but also much quieter. They were afraid their target buyers would find it boring. So they decided to make a recording of the actual exhaust sound, and then allow the driver to amplify it and play it back through the car's stereo system. No, no, no, no, one wants to say, that's not right at all! But it's best to only sigh. This is the kind of thing that's bound to happen in the final, decadent phases of the great age of the automobile.

Back in the early 2000's the people responsible for exhaust tuning at Jaguar had to deal with the fact the Jaguar really wanted to have it all. Jaguars were supposed to be elegant and luxurious, hence quiet. But certain models--including my XKR--were also supposed to be fast and sporty; hence, they had to rumble and roar a little. The result is a compromise, a car whose exhaust note is noisier than a Camry's by a long stretch but still considerably quieter than a Ferrari's or even that of a Nissan 350Z.

The issue is complicated by the fact that the XKR's engine really doesn't rev up that much. Pretty much all engines are noisier the faster they're turning. At idle--say 600 rpm--they're all pretty quiet. At higher revs, say 5000 rpm, they all tend to be a lot noisier. There is a somewhat parallel relation between rpms and power. An engine spinning at 600 rpm will have enough power to creep the car slowly forward on a level road but not enough to continue up even a slight incline. Most car engines aren't much use till they reach at least 1500 rpm and don't produce power up to their full capacity until they reach three, four, five or even six thousand rpm. The Z's motor was typical. The highest power was between 4000 and 5500 rpm. For acceleration, that's where you wanted to be. Of course it tends to be noisy up there in those high revs and since the pitch of the sound changes as the engine speeds up or slows down, whenever you're running through the gears the motor is playing quite a song for you while at the same time the acceleration is pushing you back in your seat. Noticeable stuff.

Now just as not all human singers are the same, not all engines sing the same tune in the same way. Many engines are like the Nissan's, they rev up to about 6000 rpm and then they reach their so-called red line and can't safely spin any faster. And they don't have much power way up there at their top anyway; they generate more and more horsepower as the revs rise from 1,000 to 5,000, but after about 5,500 the power starts to decline. Other engines are meant to run at lower rpm and only go up to 4000 or even just up to 3,000 before reaching their peak. Still others are designed to rev much higher. Honda and Porsche make reliable engines that go happily up to 8,000 or even 8,500. I've read that some racing engines go even higher, up above 18,000 rpm (300 revolutions per second), though it must be said that those engines are not meant to be long-lived.

The Jaguar V-8 engine has its own character. Like many others, it makes its highest power at around 5,000 rpm and does not safely operate too much faster than that. But it is designed to also produce a hefty share of its maximum power even at low revs. This is a design characteristic of the basic 4.2 liter V-8, even without the supercharger. And with a supercharger, you get even more power at low revs because increasing power down low is one of the main things that superchargers do. So yes, you can rev the Jaguar's engine up to 5,000 rpm and above, and when you do that the Jaguar is powerful and pretty noisy, the exhaust producing a deep throaty roar and the supercharger contributing its own higher pitched scream. Plenty exciting. Except that there's not much reason to ever do that. There is so much power available down in the low rpm range that you can drive all day and accelerate pretty hard with the engine still turning at only 1200 to 2700 rpm. In that rpm range the engine rumbles a little and the supercharger whines a bit, the latter mostly drowning out the former. If it sounds like anything, it sounds like a boat. A boat? I have a car that sounds like a boat? If I had wanted to listen to a boat, I'd have bought a dang boat!

To summarize, then, we have a mostly quiet engine that

sounds a little like a boat. We have a suspension that acts automatically to keep the car planted and a stability control system that prevents wheel spin. We have a six-speed automatic transmission that makes its shifts quickly, smoothly and unobtrusively. Undramatic is one word that you might use to describe this, but boring is another. So much for 'fun to drive.'

Okay, another reader might say, but it's still a Jaguar. Isn't that kind of fun in itself, tooling around in the Jag? Well, that's a good question. There's certainly a kind of aura around the name Jaguar, a brand identity as the marketers call it. But isn't that just hype? Hm. When I bought my 2004 XKR I was certainly focused on the specifications of that particular car and whether it would please me to own it, but I was also being swayed in a more general way by what I knew of the brand's history. My knowledge of old Jaguars was vague and fragmented, but I had strong positive feelings about them and that made a difference. I don't think I am the only person this has ever happened to, either in regard to Jaguar or in regard to any number of other kinds of cars. Where do these positive feelings come from? In our particular case at hand, let's take a look at the history of the Jaguar brand and see if we can figure it out.

Chapter 2: A Short History of Jaguar Cars

The first car to carry the name Jaguar was produced in 1936 by a British company called SS Cars, Ltd. The SS stood for Swallow Sidecars, which was the original name of the company when it was founded back in 1921 by two young fellows named William. When they met, William Walmsley already had a business; he was refurbishing and selling World War I surplus motorcycles. William Lyons was younger, just 20 years old, and was working as a salesman in a Sunbeam dealership. He'd been working there since he was eighteen, the year when he had finished an engineering apprenticeship at an auto manufacturer called Crossley Moters.

Crossley is not well known today in the U.S., but some readers will know the name Sunbeam. Sunbeam started out in 1888 making bicycles, but soon branched out into motorcycles and cars. In the twenties the company was quite successful but like many businesses it failed during the Great Depression, at which point its assets and brand name were purchased by the Rootes group. The Sunbeam name lived on in the Rootes-produced Sunbeam-Talbots of the late thirties and late forties. In the fifties Rootes released a series of successful sporting and racing cars, and began calling them simply Sunbeams. In America the best known of the Sunbeams were the sports cars of the 1960s, including the Sunbeam Tiger, which was created when the company hired American Carroll Shelby to fit their tiny car with a 260 cubic inch Ford V-8, the same engine that powered my mother's Mercury Comet Caliente of that same era. The Sunbeam brand was sold in 1964 to the Chrysler Corporation, who managed to destroy it. But I digress.

Back in 1921, the young Sunbeam seller William Lyons was passionate about motorcycles. He met William Walmsley when he was shopping for a sidecar. The two young men got the idea to set up a business making sidecars in volume. They had a source of capital--borrowing from their parents--but they couldn't immediately get started because Lyons was underage. On his twenty-first birthday a company was formed and named Swallow Sidecars.

Success followed and within a few years the company had expanded into building 'coachwork' for automobiles. In modern terms they were mostly just building car bodies that they could then bolt on to frames and running gear assemblies (chassis) made by others. One of their first cars involved some surplus Fiat chassis that no one else saw any use for. To reflect this new line of business, the company's name changed to Swallow Sidecars and Coachbuilding. By 1932 the company was having chassis created to their own specifications, essentially producing their own complete car. The first of these was the SS1, produced from 1932 to 1936. Fewer than ten of these cars still exist. In 2013 one well restored example came up for auction and sold for $154,000.

It was during this period that Walmsley and Lyons parted ways. The story we hear today is that there was a disagreement about whether to take the company public. Lyons was for it; Walmsley was against. To settle the matter, Lyons bought out Walmsley's share of the business in 1934. The name of the company changed again, this time to SS Cars. In the early thirties the company's cars sold well, even during the difficult economic times, due to their winning combination of beautiful styling and low cost. It was during this period that the original Sunbeam company failed. Lyons wanted to buy the remaining assets, but was outbid by Rootes.

Though his SS cars were selling reasonably well even in the midst of a depression, Lyons became concerned about criticism that they lacked power and were getting a reputation for being pretty but not serious. In response, Lyons hired a man named Harry Weslake to make him a more powerful engine. To go with the new engine Lyons created a new body design. He named the new model the SS Jaguar 100, the 100 referring to the car's claimed top speed. From that day forward, Lyons began calling all of his cars Jaguars and began emphasizing speed. If there is such a thing as the 'Jaguar aura" or the "Jaguar mystique" this is where it began. In 2010, a well-restored SS Jaguar 100 sold at Pebble Beach for $1,045,000.

During WW2 car production ceased in Britain, but Lyons and his designers spent at least part of their time in the war years working on a design for a newer, even more powerful engine that they were calling the XK. And indeed a new engine did appear in the company's first post-war sports car, the Jaguar XK 120, which debuted in 1948. By that time the SS name had been dropped due to the association with Nazi Germany and the company had become simply Jaguar Cars.

The XK 120 was very fast for its time, with a high-tech 3.4 liter engine designed by Harry Weslake and Walter Hassan. It had overhead cams and twin SU carburetors. The first XK 120 car was a one-off design, consisting of the brand new engine attached to a shortened chassis of an older Jaguar sedan, the whole thing then covered with a showy aluminum body, created by Lyons and a team of panel beaters in the space of two weeks, just in time for the 1948 London Motor Show. The idea was really just to show off the engine; there were no immediate plans to put it into a production sports car. The show car was so well received, however, that Lyons very quickly began producing it. Part of the excitement was that the claimed 120 mph top speed was higher than any other production car at that time. In fact Lyons had no proof that the car would go that fast because conditions in England at that time made full capacity testing quite difficult. The cars were soon tested, though, on a long straight road in Belgium, where they lived up to the hype and achieved 126 mph. Contemporary owners of XK 120s included three Hollywood legends: Clark Gable, Gary Cooper and Humphrey Bogart as well as the young French novelist Françoise Sagan. In 1950 the first Pebble Beach Road Race was won by an XK 120 driven by Phil Hill.

In the fifties, the XK 120 evolved into the XK 140 and XK 150 production cars and also the C-Type and D-Type racing cars. Jaguar had five wins at Le Mans: 1951, '53, '55, '56 and '57. The wins at Le Mans, which was the pre-eminent motorsport event of the time, enhanced the reputation of the cars and sales remained strong. The 1955 Le Mans race, however, was doubly tragic. At the race itself, the worst accident in motor racing history occurred when a Mercedes racecar traveling at 150 mph struck an Austin-Healey and then crashed into an embankment. The Mercedes disintegrated and some of its parts--including the hood, front axle and engine block--flew into the crowd. The driver, Pierre Levegh, and at least 79 spectators were killed. The race was won by driver Mike Hawthorn in a Jaguar D-Type. There was a shadow over this victory, however, as Hawthorn had also been involved in the accident. He had suddenly slowed down to enter the pits, taking advantage of the D-Type's four wheel disc brakes, which delivered shorter stopping distances than the drum brakes in all the other cars. Driver Lance Macklin in an Austin-Healey 100 was close behind and had to veer left to avoid hitting the Jaguar. This put him in the path of the rapidly overtaking Mercedes and also caused a brief cloud of dust to rise and possibly obscure the Mercedes driver's view. Horrific footage of the crash can be found by searching for 1955 Le Mans disaster.

Even before this, however, a more personal tragedy had struck the Lyons family when William's son John Michael was killed in a road accident while driving to Le Mans just before the 1955 race. The 1951 and 1953 wins at Le Mans had featured heavily in Jaguar marketing efforts, but the 1955 race was never mentioned. Lyons in fact soon disbanded the factory-sponsored racing team and the '56 and '57 Jaguar victories were won by an independent team based in Scotland.

The most famous Jaguar of all was the E-Type, known as the XKE in the United States. A direct descendent of the D-Type

The SS Jaguar 100, first produced in 1936, was one of the first cars to carry the Jaguar name. The 3.5 liter model could reach 100 mph.

The Jaguar XK 120 was released in 1949. It used a brand new engine called the XK.

A Short History of Jaguar Cars

The most famous Jaguar is the E-Type, produced from 1961 to 1974. The first cars used XK straight six engines; later cars got a new V-12.

The Jaguar Mark 2 was produced from 1959 to 1967. Inspector Morse had a red one in the 1987-2000 television series.

race car, the E-Type was manufactured by Jaguar from 1961 to 1974. Styling was by aerodynamic engineer Malcolm Sayer, presumably with much input from Lyons. When it was released, Enzo Ferrari himself called it 'the most beautiful car in the world." It was powered first by a triple carbureted 3.8 liter XK engine, later by a 4.2 liter XK, and still later by another legendary Jaguar motor, a new 5.3 liter V-12. Besides going fast and looking good, the E-Type had one more attractive quality: it was relatively affordable. Today we are used to thinking of Jaguars as a premium brand with premium pricing, but in the sixties Jaguars excelled as value for money cars. When new, the E-Type was cheaper than any of its direct competitors, including Porsche, Ferrari and Aston Martin. Both the E-Type sports cars and the Mark I and II sedans (saloons in Britspeak) offered luxury and performance that were at least somewhere within reach of the middle class.

This then was Jaguar's golden age, the most obvious source of the Jaguar aura of speed and grace. Famous owners of E-types included Brigitte Bardot, Tony Curtis, Steve McQueen, George Best, Frank Sinatra, Roy Orbison, Mary Tyler Moore, and Tina Turner. Besides that somewhat diverse group (Mary Tyler Moore and Tina Turner?) more than 70,000 other people bought E-Types in the sixties and seventies and millions more would have liked to. In the eighties and nineties more millions admired the red Jaguar Mark II driven by Inspector Morse in the British television series. As originally created by author Colin Dexter, Morse drove a Lancia; but when the TV series came into being, actor John Thaw saw the inspector as more of a Jaguar man.

The Jaguar golden age began to crumble in the late sixties and early seventies as the entire British car making industry began to collapse. Consolidation in the industry led to one of Jaguar's most important suppliers being purchased by a Jaguar competitor. In the face of this disaster, Lyons did not contest what was essentially a hostile takeover bid and in 1966 Jaguar became part of the British Motor Corporation (BMC). Lyons remained involved with the Jaguar division and his final accomplishment was to oversee production of the XJ6, which replaced the Mark II.

Further consolidation of the British car industry culminated in an entity called British Leyland, the same British Leyland where Triumph came to die. BL was not a success and the whole thing led to government intervention in 1975, essentially a nationalization of the company. Quality control problems, labor disputes, and general mismanagement did not end with nationalization. Jaguar sedans continued to be built and sold, but quality control was poor and prices had risen. Things began to improve in the eighties but only after a third of the Jaguar work force was laid off and the company was re-privatized. There was still no replacement of any kind for the E-Type, which had ended its production run in 1974.

Re-privatization meant that in the eighties there was a new, independent company again called Jaguar Cars. Among the many who stepped forward to buy stock in the new company was the Ford Motor Company. At this time Jaguar was positioned as a premium brand, making sporty and luxurious sedans: During its first years of independence the company made some strides, mostly by cutting costs and improving quality. In the latter part of the eighties the company returned to racing in conjunction with Tom Walkinshaw Racing. In 1989 a TWR Jaguar XJR-9 won the 24 Hours of Daytona and also won at Le Mans, breaking Porsche's string of eight straight victories there. In 1990 a Jaguar XJR-12 won again at Le Mans. But the company had trouble capitalizing on these successes as lack of cash forced delays in design and production of new consumer models. The brand began to lose ground as sales stagnated.

In 1989 Ford offered to buy out all other stockholders and by February of 1990, Jaguar was a division of Ford. Also in this era, Ford acquired Volvo, Land Rover and Aston Martin. Ford's stewardship lasted from 1990 until 2008, when the company sold all four of its European prestige brands. Cash from these sales was one factor that kept Ford afloat in 2009 when GM and Chrysler both failed.

The 2008 buyer for both Jaguar and Land Rover was the Indian carmaker Tata. Tata merged Jaguar and Land Rover, creating the JLR Group. In the years since then, JLR has done well, surprising some analysts, with sales expanding dramatically, especially in Asia. For a few years, the group continued in the Ford direction, producing new Jaguars and Land Rovers that Ford had already planned and buying Ford engines to power them. More recently the company has produced all new designs and has just released its first true sports car since the E-Type, a two-seater called the F-Type. It is a high performance--and very noisy--roadster aimed at competing with the Porsche Boxster and similar cars from BMW and Audi.

JLR currently has factories in Merseyside, Solihull, and Castle Bromwich. In August of 2013 the company announced a major expansion of the Land Rover facility in Merseyside and also increased hiring at the Solihull Jaguar plant. The company has more than 24,000 employees in the UK and is planning to open a production facility in China in 2015.

And speaking of Jaguar factories, I know that my car, like many in the Ford era, was made in two different plants. The body of my car was made at the Castle Bromwich plant near Birmingham. It was painted there and then put on a truck to carry it to the Brown's Lane plant near Coventry, where the car was assembled. This division of labor--car bodies in one plant and chassis in another--echoes the very early days when bodies were the only parts of the car that the company made.

The Brown's Lane plant was Jaguar's corporate headquarters from 1951 to 2005. It was acquired by William Lyons in 1951, when the success of his first post-war cars had encouraged him to expand. A search for a good location led him to Coventry, an area that had both manufacturing space available and a good supply of labor. At both Brown's Lane and Castle Bromwich Jaguar moved into space that during WW2 had been used for production of Supermarine Spitfire Mark II fighter planes. Brown's Lane was also the site of what was called, in capital letters, the Wood Shop, where up to 500 workers were employed just to produce wood veneers for Jaguar, Aston Martin and Land Rover. Car production at Brown's Lane ceased after 2004, making my car one of the last to be assembled there. Browns Lane was also home to the

Jaguar Heritage Museum. This has since been moved, but a virtual tour of the original museum is still available online.

The main buildings at Browns Lane were demolished in 2008. Parts of the area have been developed for residential use. In memory of the Jaguar era, one section is known as Lyons Park. Another section is called Swallow's Nest.

Chapter 3: Ambushed by a Jaguar

My 2004 car, then, is a kind of a Ford. Ford may have been an over-controlling parent in some ways, but in other respects they ran Jaguar reasonably well, providing hefty investment in new manufacturing equipment and in research and design. This expensive investment meant that Ford probably never made a profit from Jaguar, but several new models were produced and quality control increased dramatically. During the Ford era Jaguars climbed from the bottom of the heap to the highest tier in customer satisfaction surveys. Knowing this helped me to take the ominous step of returning to the world of British cars--a place which I had once sworn I would never enter again after having messed around with a TR3 (flawed but fantastic), a TR4 (flawed and semi-fantastic) and an Austin Healey Sprite (too little and too late).

Did I break my never-again-a-Britcar vow because back in the sixties I had longed for an E-Type--or XKE as it was called in the U.S.? I don't know. In the actual sixties I was a too young and too far away. There were no Jaguars around for me to admire in my town and even when I did become vaguely aware of them, they were nowhere within the financial reach of a teenager or a struggling college student. It wasn't till the eighties and early nineties that I really starting thinking how desirable E-Types were and by then they were already established classics, which is a way of saying that they were old enough to be falling apart and yet still quite expensive to buy. Even when I got a little money in the nineties, I never seriously considered a Jaguar of any sort.

As mentioned in the last chapter, the whole Jaguar enterprise was in disarray from the latter half of the seventies through most of the eighties. There was no real replacement for the E-Type when that model finally ran out of steam in 1974. Instead Jaguar produced the XJS, a glorious and powerful car that was competitive with Ferrari and Mercedes in some aspects of performance, but which was also large, heavy and expensive--a pure grand tourer.

Besides price, build quality was an issue in this era and I remember being vaguely aware of it even back then. The famous E-Type itself had not been all that well put together. An inadequate cooling system meant that the cars were prone to overheating, the brakes were not what they might have been, and the British-made wiring and electrical components were...hmm, how to put this...let's just say they were not world class. And while such flaws were somewhat acceptable in a not overly expensive sports car, the higher end grand touring market was less forgiving. Mercedes luxury cars were equally fast and comfortable, but they also had a reputation for being precise and indestructible; Jaguars did not. And since the XJS was not by any stretch a sports car, Jaguar could not compete with Porsche at all. So for a long time, as a practical matter, there was no Jaguar I wanted, even had money been no object.

That situation began to change in 1996, when Jaguar released the XK8. Ford had provided funding for Jaguar to design and build an all-new engine, just the fourth new engine design in Jaguar history, and also a new body style, long and low, elegant but fast-looking, a style that would fit right in if set down next to an E-Type, an XK 120 or an SS 100. The car was larger than these, of course, and as we have seen it was more a grand touring car than a sports car, but it was a step in the sports car direction. Then in 1997, another option appeared in the form of a supercharged XK8, which Jaguar had decided to call the XKR. With more oomph, the XKR edged a tiny bit closer to sporting territory. So, did I want one? Well, yeah, in an abstract sort of way, yes, but the price was so far out of my range that it was pointless to even think about it. And besides, at that point I was driving a Miata, one of the greatest sports cars of all time, and I was loving it.

Something must have happened, though, because Jaguar caught me in the end. And it was the brand name, the aura, that helped to reel me in. It must have been, since I'd never actually driven a Jaguar and never even been up close to the model I was interested in.

The year the Jaguar caught me was 2012. I'd worked hard and saved up a little cash, but not a whole lot, so any kind of new car was out of reach. I had to get a used car and I'd have to sell or trade my Nissan 350Z as part of the deal. Now the Z was a perfectly good car; I would recommend it to anyone. So why did I want to change cars? A reasonable question. I suppose it was because, basically, I like to change cars. Call it an endearing quirk or call it a character flaw, but there it is. Complicating things was the fact that I had decided to retire from my job. That had major bearing. I could have kept on working and saved up more money. But I figured that it would be better to retire and spend my time driving around in a pretty nice car than it would be to keep on working long enough to buy a really, really nice car and then die.

Well there are some great used cars in the world, fast interesting cars. There are Honda NSXs around, there are Lexus 400 series cars, several great BMWs with either two seats or four, a number of very nice Mercedes, and lots of Porsches. Those are all nice, and one of the Italian exotics--a Ferrari or a Lamborghini--would also have been excellent. Those last two, though, they're awfully expensive, even when used. And as far as I know, there are no Ferrari or Lamborghini mechanics anywhere within 75 miles of my town. Buying an expensive old beat-to-death Italian seemed excessively dumb.

Thinking about Italian cars, however, is always a worthwhile endeavor. Italian cars can help us, I think, in figuring out what car brands mean to us. A consideration of Ferrari illuminates all cars. On a simple level, they can function as an ideal against which other cars can be evaluated. Your car may not measure up to a Ferrari, but how close does it come? But that way of thinking is actually a little too simple. These Italian exotics have a personality, and understanding their personality can help us understand the personality of other cars, which in turn might help us in our search for a car whose personality matches our own. So I'll start by trying to characterize Ferrari (not the car itself actually but rather the hazy image that surrounds it) and then I'll go on to some other cars that contrast with Ferrari.

I must apologize if any parts of my brand descriptions seem crudely put or perhaps a little ridiculous. It's difficult to describe the personality of cars. We are speaking of the intersection of mechanics and emotion and we don't really have a language for that. Now possibly some people might say that the challenge of describing a car's personality, the real reason we don't have a language for it, is that we're trying to describe something that doesn't exist. It's just metal, rubber and plastic, goes this reasoning. It's just a machine. Despite its commonsensical sound, however, that view is not correct. A clothes washer may be a machine, and so may a coffee grinder or an automatic paper towel dispenser. But a car radically changes one of the most basic things about you--how your body moves through space. A car vastly increases the amount and weight of things that you can carry from one place to another. It shrinks, by whole orders of magnitude, the time it takes you to get from the place you're in now to another place where you might want to be. Most of all, it simply lets you move faster, quite a lot faster than your body alone can move. It exponentially expands the area of space within which it is practical for you to travel. Your cerebral cortex may take this in stride, but the deep brain always knows that something magic is going on. And as always with magic, there are choices to be made about what sort of magic suits us. Remember the sorting hat in the first Harry Potter book? Whether we choose our type of magic or whether the magic chooses us is hard to say, but choices are made, and there are always some reasons for our choices that go beyond the rational counting of the beans.

And not only are our choices not necessarily rational, they

are also fraught with meaning. However they get made, they are not trivial. They express both what we are and what we are not. If you have chosen a Corvette, you have also not chosen a Porsche, a Mustang or a minivan. And since cars are large and obvious things, everyone is going to know what you've chosen! It's terribly embarrassing to choose a Jaguar. That's probably the main reason they depreciate so fast. But I digress. Back to Ferrari.

Italian sports cars strive to be powerful and stylish. All sports cars do that to an extent, but the Italians go the furthest. New Ferrari designs may be quite different from previous ones; the idea is to stand out, to cause a sensation. They're not modest, and they're not afraid to look ridiculous. They are exuberant; they want you to smile. The Italian ideal is that not only are you faster than anyone else around the track, you also look better than anyone else as you go. It may seem at times that they are not serious, but this is an illusion. Under the hood they are deadly serious, the product of thousands of hours of design and development; the looks may get noticed, but the look would be nothing without the performance. They are striking and beautiful; they are too flashy to be elegant, but they are hyper-stylish. Ferraris strive to go somewhere beyond what you have ever seen in a car before. Lamborghinis look for the space just on the other side of that, where you're not quite sure if it's even a car at all--or at least they used to, before the Audi era. Both cars are for people who want to be seen, seen and compared, and who want to win that comparison. Of course such people may be as insecure as you or me, but the cars make them look like they're not worried at all.

Porsches have a different personality, a more conservative one. It's acceptable for new Porsche designs to be just variations on previous ones. The Porsche 911 has had the same basic shape for fifty years now. This means endless refinement and improvement. The Italians want to be fantastic; Porsches want to be perfect. Porsches are good-looking cars, but Porsche design emphasizes power and purpose over beauty. They look plain next to Ferraris, but they don't look slow and they don't look mechanical. Porsches are not stylish in the sense of this year's fashion, but they have an organic, animal pose and a shape that echoes the feel of our own major muscle groups. Porsches are also about control. They are trophies, but they are also highly precise tools, deluxe high-end tools that give you everything you need to do the job exactly right, provided of course that you are a properly skilled operator. The joys of the Porsche may seem dry and technical, but a true craftsman understands the pure pleasure of using a tool so perfectly suited to the task. The Porsche's emotions are complex and mostly submerged. There is a hint of anger there somewhere, of impatience with the rest of the world, or perhaps of frustration that true perfection is never attained.

Mercedes Benz cars look solid and substantial. They make it clear that their owners have achieved a certain level of financial stability and well-being. The car rewards that achievement with speed, precise controls and a luxury interior. They are a bit decadent, because no good bourgeois really needs such a car, but a little comfort is well deserved. The cars are also a bit fortress-like, so as to reassure owners that their assets are protected. (Mercedes Benz is a big company and makes a huge range of vehicles, lots of them colorless and appliance-like, but here I am speaking of their upper middle level cars.)

BMWs also mark a level of financial well-being, but a lesser one and one that does not take itself quite as seriously. They seek a more enthusiastic driver and promise to make driving a spirited adventure. Their sedans are styled to look not all that different from other sedans and that's part of the point. Look at me, they say, I look like your car and I can do whatever it does for you--but I can do it better. BMW defines the category of sports sedan. The BMW roadster--the Z-4--is more highly styled than their sedans though not extremely so. It's a pretty car and even slightly whimsical, again taking itself a bit less seriously than the other Germans while trusting us to know by the BMW badge that the car will be fast, precise and refined.

Japan has produced a host of sports cars, with all the major makers trying their hand. Japanese sports car styling is oddly conservative. The cars are good-looking but rarely beautiful.

What they are is accessible, more accessible to more people. In a sense, their claim is that you can have a car that has all the fun, all the quality, and all the performance of an expensive car and which is maybe even more reliable than that expensive car, all for a reasonable price. They have been able to make good on this promise on many occasions. In the nineties the Honda NSX had all the performance of a Ferrari at a much lower price point. In 2003, when I was shopping for roadsters, it was clear that the Japanese Nissan 350Z was easily equal to base engine versions of the Porsche Boxster and BMW Z-4 roadsters. There was no practical justification whatever for the extra $10,000 that the latter two would cost. And indeed, in that same era, the Mazda RX-8 and the Honda S2000 offered a comparable experience at an even lower price. Buying a Japanese car, therefore, can be seen as the smart thing to do.

So why doesn't everyone buy Japanese? I think it's because the whole notion of 'just as good but cheaper' is self-defeating. It's hard for us to really believe it, even when it's objectively true. And of course it sometimes isn't quite true. The Honda NSX was as fast as a Ferrari, but there's a lot more to being a Ferrari than that, not least of which was that the Ferrari was beautiful while the NSX looked kind of dorky. My 2004 350Z was faster on the track than certain 2004 Porsches and BMWs costing thousands more, but the savings came from using parts made for other Nissan cars, mostly bigger cars. It had a nice big engine to move those heavy parts around, but the whole thing was a little heavier, a little more muscle-bound than the others. Is that a big problem? That depends on you. I think it's a wonderful car, but it's wonderful on its own terms; it's not the same as anything.

The most successful Japanese sports car is the Mazda MX-5, called the Miata in the U.S. It's a modern version of small, fun sports cars like the Triumph, the MG, the Fiats and the Alfa Romeos--just as much fun, still pretty cheap, and much more reliable. No one has been able to equal it. It's not "just as good but cheaper." Like the Honda Accord and Toyota Camry, it's more like "as good or better and lasts a lot longer." But also like those cars, the Miata's styling is distinctly middle of the road.

An early 90's Honda NSX photographed in 2009 by Charles01. One distinctive feature is the car's 360 degree visibility from the driver's seat.

This 90's era Lamborghini Diablo, on the other hand, seems to have little outward visibility in any direction. Other drivers are free to notice it, though, a point well made by Sujit Kumar in this 2007 photo.

This 1992 Miata shows its conservative Japanese styling. It's not a movie star, more like the guy or girl next door. This one is probably a guy, since the front and rear socks don't match.

A 2004 Nissan 350Z Roadster. Designed by Ajay Panchal at Nissan Design America in San Diego, its styling mixes a few traditional Datsun elements with hints of American muscle and a little something from the 2nd generation Audi TT.

And now, after all this exposition, what can we say about Jaguars? That is, what is the Jaguar identity and how does it differ from those others? Now I could just say that I've given you some history and some pictures, and you should just go ahead and decide for yourself, which, hopefully, you already have. But to stop there would be cheating, so I'll give it a go as the Brits say. Jaguars want to be fast and beautiful, but more than beautiful they want to be elegant. They are never crude, but they are slightly disreputable. You can't drink alcohol in a Porsche for the same reason you shouldn't drink while running a lathe. You can't drink alcohol in a Ferrari because you're too busy flying around looking good and you might spill something on your shirt. You can have a drink or two in a Mercedes, especially while being chauffeured, once you've obtained the appropriate glassware. But in a Jaguar it is permissible to drink directly from the bottle, provided only that the bottle is a reasonably good quality champagne. Jaguars are like the Italian cars in not wanting to appear too serious and in wanting to make you smile. But they are not really exuberant and it's a bit of a quieter smile at least until the champagne takes hold. If Porsches are for craftsmen, Mercedes are for business people and Ferraris are for actors and artists, who are Jaguars for? Jaguars are for people of means whose sources of income are not clear, possibly because they have something to hide or possibly because they have inherited wealth and do no useful work at all. Now this doesn't at all describe me. But does it describe someone I might want to be? Sigh. I warned you it was embarrassing.

In my defense, I only realized this later. When I bought the car, I was just clueless.

Chapter 4: The J Gate

It's bad enough that my new Jaguar showed up in my driveway with an automatic transmission, but at least that was expected. What I hadn't realized was that it had the infamous Jaguar J Gate shifter, one of the many things I was clueless about. When I first saw it, I didn't mind it at all. I thought it was kind of cool. It had two separate sections. Park, reverse, neutral, and drive were on one side; gears two through five were on the other. That seemed sort of logical. I doubted I'd ever use the numbered gear selector side though because what was the point of doing manually what the car would do for you? I had always liked manuals, but I had known going in that Jaguar didn't make one and I was resigned to it.

What a fool I was! I needed my consciousness raised, to become aware that the J Gate was one of the worst of Jaguar's sins. I wasn't supposed to be resigned; I was supposed to be pissed off. Here's just a sample of what experts were saying:

> *To shift the six-speed automatic yourself, you must use Jaguar's clunky, long-in-the-tooth J-gate shifter. (Hint: It's not worth it.)*   -Road and Track

> *The J-gate is slow to pick up a gear and it is difficult to tell which one it will hit without the driver glancing down.*
>   -drive.com.au

It's time for someone to take the J-gate out back and shoot it. -Automobile Magazine

As I read more and more about Jaguars of my era, it seemed after a while that all the automobile journalists of the world had gotten together and drafted a short list of approved adjectives to describe the J Gate. "Clunky" and "long-in-the-tooth" were both on the list, and the most positive allowable adjective was "venerable," a word that seemed to mean "at one time possibly worthy of respect for reasons no one can remember, but now both useless and ridiculous." And then I ran across this reference, specifically to a 2004 Jaguar:

"Jaguar thankfully kept its trademark J-Gate..."

Wait a minute. I didn't think "trademark" was even on the list of adjectives. And what's up with "thankfully?" What raving lunatic wrote this? Ah yes, JaguarLovers.com. They must be, like, goofballs or something.

Despite knowing how useless it was, I started to play with it a little anyway. And I had a revelation. Using those numbered gears on the left side of the shifter is a little weird, but it can be a lot of fun. It doesn't change your car into a manual and the writer at drive.com in Australia is correct that the J Gate does not pick up the new gear quickly. But what it will do is help you keep the revs up. Let's say you're driving along at a legal speed of say 60 mph and you see a curve coming. You're going to slow down a bit because even though the Jag could easily just continue on through the curve at 60, you might scare the other drivers and besides it's a blind curve and, who knows, there might be a deer or a kid or something around the other side. And besides that, remembering the famed advice of Jackie Stewart, the thing you really like about curves is going in slowly and coming out fast. So. Your car has either a five speed or a six-speed automatic and as you brake and enter the curve, the transmission is in top gear and your revs are around 1500 rpm or even lower. Now the thing is, this is not a race and the

The J Gate may be old tech, but it is still functional and attractive. And hey, J is for Jaguar. Was Mercedes ever able to develop an M Gate? Did Porsche even dare attempt a P Gate? No and no. Were those failures due to lack of technical ability? Or was it because those companies just weren't cool enough?

The J Gate

Jaguar motors have plenty of low-end torque, so you don't need to be at 5000 rpm to accelerate nicely out of the curve, but you do need at more than 1500. You need to be somewhere around 3000. If you let the car do it, you'll stay in top gear until you stomp on it coming out. The car will hiccup a bit. It knows it has to shift but first it wonders if the next gear down might be low enough. But of course it isn't, so then it shifts into the next lower or maybe even the next. This doesn't take too long--less time than it takes to describe in fact--but it takes long enough to be really annoying. When I describe my Jaguar as a lazy car--lazy just like most live cats are lazy--this is one thing I'm talking about.

But let's go back a minute, suppose the car is not in sixth when you stomp on the gas. Suppose it's already in fourth or third because you put it there with the J Gate. When you did that, when you pushed the shifter over the left from drive and then up a notch or two, the change from sixth to fourth didn't happen instantly. No, not at all. But it didn't really matter because on the way into a curve such crispness isn't as critical. The point is that when you are ready to really push out of the curve and go, your revs are already up and the car's response is much quicker than in the first scenario.

Even better, when the road is more curvy than straight, don't bother with your top gear at all. Depending on the road, you can drive basically in fourth, with third for some corners and fifth for straights. The Jaguar is not a racer; it's a grand tourer. It's got an automatic transmission and the actuation is the old fashioned kind. But you can have a lot of fun with the J Gate.

One final bit of advice. What if you're just trying to accelerate from zero to 60 or whatever? Should you use the J Gate? Well, it's kind of interesting to do that but also kind of pointless. When it's just a matter of running up the gears, the Jaguar transmission is a jewel. Just leave it in Drive with the sport button on and put your foot down. It's a beautiful world. And if for some reason you don't like the world at 60, just wait for 120; it won't take long.

What I have come to believe is that J Gate is a kind of red

herring. Some people complain that it's hard to use because you have to look down; and others complain that the detents are not solid enough. (So make up you minds, critics: is it too clunky or not clunky enough? Jeez.) But all these complaints are just quibbling. If you really like manuals and you get an automatic, you're going to be disappointed. The shape of the shift gate is not really the problem. Similarly, if you're interested in crisp, clutchless paddle shifting, you're going to be disappointed again. Going forward, yes, there is new technology that is superior. By 2011 even the Mazda 3 had a more effective manumatic mode than the old J Gate. The quote from Automobile magazine is from 2009, a point in time when Jaguar was very obviously lagging in technology as compared to its play group. By then though, Jaguar was already taking the magazine's advice. As of this writing, newer Jags have paddle shifters and the J Gate is no more.

So my car is a bit on the old tech side and might be the subject of derision from Porsche owners. But you may have noticed that I have kind of given up on trying to convince you how crappy it is. I've actually admitted that you can have some fun driving it. It took me a while to get to this point. I got the car in the summer of 2012 and spent the following winter moaning about wheels and how expensive they are to repair and about how the Jaguar wasn't really sporty enough. Winters here are not cold, but they are long and wet and gray. I drove the car rarely and when I did I found myself unconsciously driving too slow for traffic. What was that? What a lazy car! Blah-blah-blah. Then one day sometime late in the spring of 2013 I noticed that the sun had come out. I started tooling around in the Jaguar with the top down. Soon I was beginning to see life differently. This car really drives well and it's really comfortable. The miles just disappear. And if you want to, you can pass just about everybody. Why bother fixing the wheels at all? Who cares about appearance or collectability? Who cares about the price? Let's get out and drive! Yes, my cheap tires are less than perfect, but they're not terrible.

I began to appreciate the effortlessness of the Jag, the big reserve of power that lurked beneath the surface, waiting for someone to seriously ask to go fast. I was starting to have a little more respect for the computer active suspension. It really does change the car's character depending on what the driver is asking the car to do. Cruising along at lowish speeds? The car is smooth and soft. It feels, in fact, like the kind of car that you maybe wouldn't want to go too fast in, especially around a curve. It would probably roll or skid or at least squeal. But then, suppose you go fast anyway, suppose you go around a curve considerably faster than the yellow sign suggests. Suddenly the car is taut and sure-footed, just what you want when you're going around a curve. And, not only is it going fast, it's making it seem pretty easy, like maybe you could even go faster if you were so inclined. Hmm.

But before we get going too fast, we need to consider the legalities. Are we going to stay on public roads or are we going to a racetrack? Also, how suicidal are we? What's the relationship between illegal speeds and dangerous speeds? One of my students bought a new Mustang and while driving it home from the dealer got himself cited for going 110 mph and for not having insurance. He didn't hurt himself or anyone else, but even so the fine was really high. It's always better to stay on the right side of the law if possible. But is it really possible for a normal American driver to drive at no more than the allowed 7.5 mph over the speed limit all the time, forever and ever, in all situations? Even worse, what happens to normal American drivers who somehow find themselves driving Jaguars? And what happens if you get stopped for speeding and you also have another problem, like for example you're missing a front license plate? Things can get complicated.

Chapter 5: The License Plate Problem

Even though we started out about 700 miles away from each other, getting possession of my new Jaguar was pretty easy. As I mentioned in the Introduction, I sent this fellow in California some money, then he had one of his people drop the Jag off in my driveway and drive back to California in my 350Z. Well, that was cool, but there were some paperwork and DMV formalities in both states that didn't get done very fast. More about that later. It meant that I was driving around for three months or so with no license plates, just a little folded up piece of paper from the California DMV stuck to the inside of the windshield on the passenger side. That gave me three whole months to contemplate the fact that the car had no obvious mounting point for a front license plate. No problem in the rear, there was a nice obvious place back there. But in the front? No sign.

Are front license plates really necessary? Most people don't give this issue much thought, possibly because they have lives. But certain others, discerning and thoughtful individuals in almost all cases, have noticed that some cars look much better without front license plates and have questioned whether we really need them. Most of us are okay with rear plates. We want people to remember the number of a car pulling away from a crime; we want to easily identify stolen cars; we want

The License Plate Problem

our police to be able to track down the number of a car they are following. Rear plates are definitely ugly, but they do accomplish those worthy goals. What do front plates do? Do we really need the opportunity to jot down the number of the car that is rushing towards us, about to run us down? No. That would be dumb. Are we worried about clever criminals reversing away from the scene of a crime? I don't think so. Can we figure out the license number of a car that is following us by reading their front plate in our rearview mirror? Nah, everything's backwards; it's too hard to figure it out and drive at the same time. So why do we have front plates? Is there any evidence that front plates improve public safety in any way? Hmm. Twenty-nine states require front plates and twenty-one states do not. Are people in the twenty-nine front plates states any better off? That seems very doubtful. The only thing we know for sure is that in the twenty-one states with no front license requirement, cars like the 2004 Jaguar XKR are quite attractive from the front and their owners are happy and content. Are there any car owners in those same twenty-one states who are unhappy and discontented by reason of being deprived of front plates? This seems unlikely. The conclusion is clear. Front plates are of dubious value at best; the twenty-nine states that require them are wasting time, effort and money. Which is, of course, a natural thing for humans to do once they get in groups and start trying to organize things. Can anything be done about this? In general, I am not optimistic.

Unfortunately for me, Oregon is one of the twenty-nine states in which front plates are required. Originally, though, my car was registered in California, and when it arrived here it didn't come with a front plate holder of any kind or with any visible bracket to mount one on. That was fine with me at first, since I didn't want a front plate there anyway. And it caused me to assume that California was one of the states that did not require front plates. But then I learned that California does require fronts, so I had to wonder what was going on. Did the former owner simply flout the law? Or did he mount a front plate but then remove all traces of what he had done when it was time to sell? There really were no traces of any U.S. style plate that I can see. If you look at the photo of the Jag's front grill, one thing you might notice is that there just isn't any obvious place to mount a license plate. Whatever you do, you almost have to block the grill, which is also the air intake for the cooling system and surely we wouldn't want that. So are Jaguars simply made not to have front plates? Well, actually, they are designed to have front plates, but not the plates we are familiar with. The mounting points don't show in the photo, but it turns out that there are some license plate brackets hiding behind the mesh grill. They're not immediately helpful because they're sized for European style plates, which are long and narrow, a totally different shape from American ones. So there was no way I could just screw on an American style holder even if I wanted to, which, as you may remember, I didn't.

So when I got my two regulation Oregon license plates, I mounted one on the back and put the other in the trunk. It was sort of like a spare. If the other one happened to blow off something, I'd still be good, which I figured was really kind of cool. It's not everyone who can say that they carry a spare license plate for emergencies. Of course I was not technically in compliance with local law, but how important could that be? A neighbor assured me that he had been going without front plates on his Cadillacs for many years in Oregon and had never had any trouble. Also on the plus side, I figured that if I wanted to visit my friends in Arizona I was totally good to go, especially if I went via Nevada.

All was well for about six months. But then came a beautiful spring day when I was driving around doing all sorts of law-abiding citizen type errands. At one point I was going along a narrow residential street. This happened to be a street near a high school baseball field and there was a game going on. A police car coming in the other direction had stopped more or less in the middle of the street. Since there were cars parked on both sides of the street, there was no way I could get through unless the police car moved. The officer was just sitting in there, looking long and hard at a car that was parked half into a driveway, blocking the sidewalk and sticking out a little into

The License Plate Problem

Front view of new/used Jaguar as delivered. Say what you like about the look, adding a front license plate is not going to improve it.

Proper placement of front license plate in normal situations. Useful in case rear plate falls off the back of the trunk lid and is lost. Narrow packet on right holds zip ties.

the street. I'm pretty sure the cop was contemplating whether or not to cite the car for improper parking. I further surmise that he finally decided that they were here for the game and it wasn't that bad, so he could just let it go. Then he saw me in my noticeable car with the top down just a few yards in front of him with no visible front license plate. He pulled up next to me and spoke to me out of his window. I needed to get that front plate on there, he said. He promised that if he ever saw me again without it, he'd give me a ticket. I said I understood.

This event meant that I could no longer just enjoy the looks of my new car's plateless front end with no thought to the law. Ah the great virtues of denial! Alas for the ending of a golden age of bliss! I had to do something, but what? Giving in, of course, would be the simplest solution, as it always is. Maybe I should just mount the front plate and be done with it. That would be sensible, but also depressing. Did I have any other realistic options, other than making a major change to my address? Hm. Must think.

First, I decided to gather some evidence about the scale of this issue. I started looking around to see if there were any other cars out there driving around in Oregon without front license plates. In fact I got kind of obsessive about it and for a week or so every time I went down the road I would be scanning every oncoming car to see if it had front plates. This is not safe driving practice, by the way. You can't actually scan all oncoming traffic for the presence of license plates and watch where you're going at the same time. Eventually I had to give it up.

But I engaged in this risky behavior long enough to notice that there were a considerable number of vehicles driving through my town that are not wearing front license plates. I didn't keep an exact record, but I'm pretty sure that if we got all serious and scientific about this, we would find out that two or three cars out of every hundred are out of compliance. Two or three percent may not sound like a lot at first, but consider how many cars there are out there. Even in my small town, the number of cars is in the tens of thousands, which means that the number without front plates is in the hundreds. So I was not alone. I also noticed--and this is just an impression--that many of the vehicles without front plates are luxury cars, sports cars or pickups. I was especially struck by the number of late model Mercedes in the group. But I digress. In any case it was clear that enforcement of the front plate requirement was not absolute by any means. I was happy to see this, and not just for myself. I liked the idea that law enforcement personnel in my area might be a little reluctant to spend time on a minor infraction of a pointless law.

I might pause here for another kind of confession. I am of a certain race and I live in a little bubble of a college town. Judging from the experience in our great United States as a whole, if I were of another race and living in a another town, I would probably have been wise to slap on that front plate on day one, end of story.

Of course I would have been wise to slap that plate on anyway, because now I was afraid to even go to town in case I ran into that same officer again. I figured that even if he didn't really want to ticket me, he would have to because he had committed to it. I wondered briefly if there was some way I could get hold of the duty roster at the cop shop. Then maybe I could come to town only when that particular patrolman was off duty. But that was a real fantasy, especially since I didn't know his name.

Now he was a municipal officer and I live a little outside the city, so one solution to this problem would be to simply avoid taking the Jaguar to town. I have an alternate vehicle, a 1989 Corolla. It's not quite the same, but it would get me to town and back. I could drive the Jaguar out in the country, which is more fun anyway, and I could take it on trips. I might, theoretically, get stopped anywhere in the state, but the chances of that happening were fairly low and even if I were stopped it could well end with just a warning, as had this first encounter. I tried this idea for a week, while I was considering my options, but it didn't really work. Avoiding town was just too onerous. I like driving the Jag into town once in a while and so does my spouse and companion. Hmm.

Another option was just to continue on living life as I

pleased, flouting the law and dealing with the consequences whatever they might be. With luck I might be able to go on for quite some time with no further problems. If I did get ticketed, I could just pay the damn fine and go on from there. Even better, I could ask for a court date. I probably wouldn't win, but I could have my say and there was a good chance of getting the fine reduced a little if the judge was impressed. It would also take up everybody's time, and that too would be making a point. And if they were smart, they would probably realize that if I got ticketed again, I could come in and argue it again till they got really tired of me. I'm retired and I've got the time. I could offer to give them a PowerPoint. I could show a map of the twenty-one states that don't require front plates and show statistics about how crime rates and traffic accidents are no worse there than in the other twenty-nine. I could tell them about all the other cars that I had seen without front plates. I'd ask whether all those drivers were getting citations or was it just me. That would show 'em. I could talk about the role of government in a free society, about how to create the greatest good for the greatest number. The judge and the prosecutor would be thinking "Geez Louise, I went through four years of law school for this?" And at that point I would look at them and say "Yes, this is what your life has come to. We all have youthful dreams, but for you it has all come down to listening to some old guy go on and on about front license plates. But don't worry, I only have three more major points I need to make...or you could just dismiss this case now and make me disappear as if I had never been. Think about it."

    But in the end, I decided that this too was a fantasy. It's true that I am retired and have some free time. But did I really want to spend it in the county courthouse? Did I really want to make that PowerPoint? No. I decided to give in and mount a front plate, but only on my own terms. What I really needed, I decided, was a way to mount a front plate for some occasions--like driving into a possibly hostile jurisdiction--while at the same time being able to dismount the front plate for other occasions--like driving pretty much everywhere else. Okay, that sounded good, but how do you do that? For Corvettes you

The License Plate Problem

can buy a special kit to solve the problem, but it's expensive and anyway nothing similar seems to exist for the XKR. Could I make something myself? Uh...maybe.

The project would have certain basic requirements. First, there could be no drilling as this would definitely degrade both the car's looks and its value. Second, attaching and reattaching had to be relatively quick and easy. Third, when attached, the front plate had to be reasonably secure; we don't want it falling off in the grocery store parking lot or getting blown off at high speeds. Fourth, although it can block the air intake grill to some extent, this should be minimized. Fifth, the plate must not be mounted so low that it scrapes on the ground. Sixth it must be visible and readable in the judgment of the average enforcement agent. And finally, the car's looks have to be respected; the mounted plate shouldn't look too tacky and with the plate removed the car should look absolutely stock.

As is often the case with technical projects, the various requirements tend to be in conflict. The no drilling requirement, for example, makes it just a little bit harder to satisfy any of the other requirements. The need for easy on and off conflicts with the need to be secure and solid. And the fourth and fifth requirements are also in conflict because any mounting that was low enough to avoid blocking the airflow would be so low it might hit the ground or so slanted as to be invisible. A nightmare.

But as Henry Ford suggested, let's take it step by step. The ideal location is actually fairly clear. There is a point where the plate would be mounted high enough for good ground clearance and reasonable visibility but low enough not to block the airflow unduly, not any more, say, than would the long narrow Europlate that presumably the Jag is designed for.

The next question was how to attach the plate. One sub-question was whether to use a plate frame or to just mount the plate bare. My first thought was that a frame would look better, so I went out and bought one. That was a mistake; it was dumb to do that before I had solved the main question of how to attach the thing. I thought of wiring it on or of using bungee cord. The bungee idea was especially intriguing because it seemed to offer the possibility of extraordinary ease of removal and re-attachment. It was potentially pretty ugly though. The real problem was that everything used to attach the plate had to be hidden, at least from the casual glance. Adhesive velcro seemed like a possibility. But even though they have those new adhesive strips that supposedly leave no mark when they are removed, I found that a little hard to believe. And besides, the geometry of the situation didn't lend itself to a velcro solution. Or if it did, I couldn't see it.

As the photos show, my final solution involved zip ties. The ties are threaded through the grill but it's not the grill that holds them on because behind the grill the ties are also threaded through the hidden brackets that provide anchor points for mounting the European style plates of the Jaguar's home environment. The ties themselves are not reusable. To dismount the plates, I just cut the ties. To remount I use a new pair; they're cheap. This was all fairly simple; the only challenge was how to thread the ties securely onto the plate, and for that I bought some little brackets meant for who knows what and bent them till they suited my purposes. I ditched the plate frame, partly because it added weight but mostly because it looked stupid when the plates were slanted down and back at the angle I wanted. With the plates mounted, the effect is a little tacky but not so bad that it reaches out and grabs you. And the best part, to my mind, is that the placement of the front plate low down and slanting backward makes it a little less obtrusive than it might be.

So if by chance you ever face a similar problem, my advice is zip ties and polystyrene. And if you don't like the looks of my solution--which is not totally impossible because as we know there's no accounting for taste--a computer search for 'removable license plates' will get dozens or hundreds of results showing different solutions. You are not alone.

The License Plate Problem

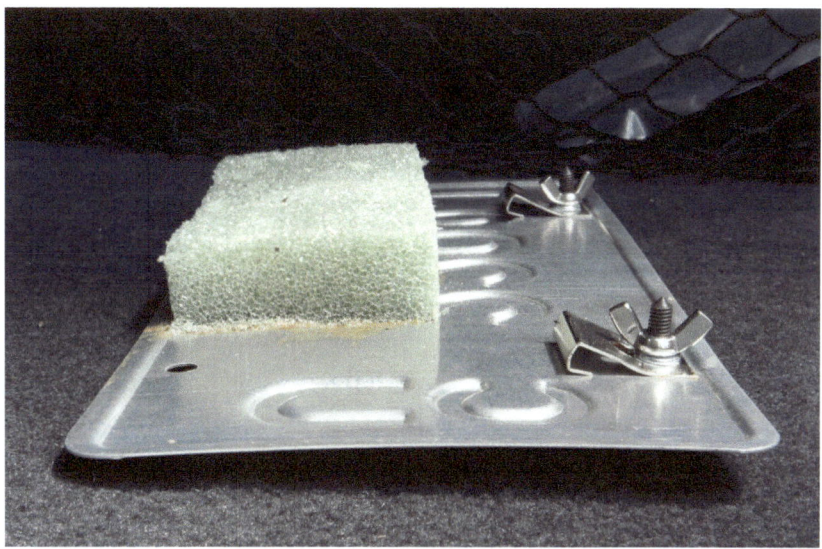

Homemade eyelets for the zip ties; polystyrene spacer to create proper angle and to stop plate from flapping around too much.

Use of hefty Jaguar logo license plate bolts helps create the illusion that plate attachment via zip ties is not a kludge. Maybe.

Confessions of a Jaguar Owner

The zip ties are invisible except from directly above. Only 10 inches of tie is used, but 14 inchers make installation easier. Excess is trimmed.

With front plate temporarily secured to front grill, the car is now reasonably secure even in dangerous neighborhoods.

Chapter 6: Speed

But enough with bureaucracy. Let's throw away the license plates for the moment and just talk about going fast. Imagine rushing along a mostly empty road, somewhere off the freeway, away from the towns. Concentrate on what's happening. You're going maybe 60 miles an hour. Whatever vehicle it is, you're not in nature anymore; you're not standing on two feet like a human being. On the one hand, you're static, trapped sitting down in a box, but at the same time you're dynamic, you're moving faster than any human can naturally move. The world is all around you, but you're not really in it, not exactly. You can see it, and sometimes you can smell it, but not in the same way you can when you just stand on your feet like a human. It's more like a film as the scenery rolls by. But you're not just watching a movie of the scenery; you are actively engaged and involved in something. What you're dealing with is the thing that mediates between you and the real world, the thing that allows you to go so inhumanly fast and that will also kill you if you mismanage it.

You might be driving an old flat bed truck with a tired motor and a noisy exhaust, the kind of truck that's a lot happier doing forty-five than it is doing sixty. The engine kind of whines and complains at sixty. You can hear it through the wind noise; and if you're an older driver, you might feel sympathetic and slow down a bit, assuming you have no pressing deadline. If you're a younger driver, you might not notice either the wind noise or the engine's sound of complaint. You might be thinking of other things entirely; you probably have some music playing. Even if you do hear the old engine whining, you're as likely to curse it as to be sympathetic. And you're more likely to either have or imagine that you have that pressing deadline, and here you are stuck in this slow old truck.

Or let's say you're in a different vehicle, a newer car, maybe a sedan, possibly a coupe but coupes are rare, so more likely an SUV or a crossover. You're going a little faster maybe, let's say 65 or so in this 55 zone. There's a little wind noise and you can hear the engine if you listen, but the sounds seem far away. You have a nice stereo that'll play music from your iPod or your phone. Or maybe you like audio books. You've got climate control. All in all, you're pretty comfortable. If it's a long drive, your muscles will be a little stiff when you finally get out, but during the drive you'll have time to think, time to enjoy the conversation of the folks in the car with you, or maybe to be annoyed or angered by your companions if that's how it's going that day.

But whatever you're thinking, the landscape still goes by like a film. Out west where I live it might be mostly rangeland and telephone poles. There would be a few ranch houses, generally off a goodly distance from the main road. Let's imagine some wide flat plains with a shallow lake but also some strange flat topped hills formed from ancient lava flows. At one point a mostly straight road might turn all curvy as you pass between the edge of the lake on your right and the base of the hills on the left. Eventually you'll have to cross one of those mesas. Your road will climb up one side, flatten out for a moment, and then fall away down the other.

I just said you had time to think; but of course if you're the driver, you have to keep some part of your mind devoted to the task at hand. You have to pay attention. You have to steer, and slow down for curves, and watch for animals or children in the road. You have to watch out for speed traps and you have to slow down a lot if you drive through a town. If you were on a freeway, you'd have other things to worry about, like when to change lanes and what exit to take and which route might have the least traffic. But like I said, we're on a smaller road now, away from the towns and the traffic is light. But still you have to pay attention. And the basic, primal reason that you have to pay attention is that going 65 miles an hour is dangerous, dangerous to you and your passengers and also dangerous to anyone you might come into contact with as you're going along.

I once read a statistic about vehicle accidents and speed. Some safety group had done research that showed that speed was a "contributing factor" in something like 88% of all accidents. Now you could interpret that as nanny talk: don't ever run with scissors and don't ever drive fast. But if you think about it, the figure is suspect. Shouldn't it be closer to 100%? Chances are very good that if you're sitting in your car in your driveway with the engine off and the car in park, you're not going to hit anything. And it's unlikely that anybody is going to hit you either. Nor is it likely that you'll go rolling down an embankment and burst into flames. Movement is the problem, our own movement and the movements of others. A man I used to know was very seriously injured in an accident one time. He was an engineer at Thiokol Corporation, the place where they made booster rockets for the Space Shuttle program, the place where they put in those infamous O-rings. The facility was way out in the boonies, miles from any town-- either for secrecy or in case it blew up--so the commute was long. There were four guys in the carpool. They were headed in to a very early shift, so they were driving through the darkness well before dawn. The car was a VW beetle, one of the original kind. They were going maybe 50 or 60--their true speed I don't really know--when they hit a black cow that was walking across the road. The two men in front were killed, the two in the rear seriously injured. Was speed a contributing factor? Yes, son, it was. If they'd been walking to work, going say, three miles per hour like a natural human animal, they would have seen, or smelled, or heard the cow and tragedy would have been avoided. This accident was before the era of airbag and these days the men in the car may have been better off. But even today, you do not want to hit a cow at speed.

So speed is dangerous, and in a general way, we assume that the higher the speed the more danger there is. This last idea is a simplistic one, and in its purest form seems incontrovertible. Let's say a cow appears in the road 50 feet in front us. Let's say we're going 10 miles per hour. How many seconds do we have to react and make sure we don't hit the cow? Ten mph equals about 14.5 feet per second. Fifty feet divided by 14.5 fps equals about 3.5 seconds. If we're paying attention, 3.5 seconds is probably long enough for us to notice the cow and react and for our car's brakes to stop the car. But 10 mph isn't very fast. Let's add some speed. Now let's say we're going 60 miles an hour, which is considered to be a reasonably safe highway speed. Sixty mph is about 87 feet per second. Fifty feet divided by 87 is .57, which means we have just a little more than half a second to not hit the cow. Hm. Sounds like trouble. How about if we're going 100 mph and that same imaginary cow suddenly appears that same 50 feet in front of us? One hundred mph equals about 145 feet per second. Fifty feet divided by 145 fps is .35, just a bit more than a third of a second. Oh dear, that is not going to do it. The top speed of many Jaguars is 155 mph. At that speed the time to avoid the cow drops to .22, less than a fourth of a second. The imaginary cow, the imaginary car and the imaginary driver are all in big trouble, and in fact they've been in big trouble ever since the car got up to much more than that original 10 mph.

Before leaving this little thought experiment behind, it wouldn't hurt to examine some of the assumptions involved and some of variables that we might have to consider if we want to apply this lesson to the real world. To begin with, we've more or less assumed that the cow is standing directly across our lane on a two-lane road. The other lane has oncoming traffic, coming fast, so we can't swerve around the cow to the left. To the right there's some sort of cliff, a hundred foot drop off to some rocks below, so we can't swerve that way either. In this scenario, the only thing we can do is put on the brakes and stop. (Now, in this situation, you might be asking, how the heck did a cow come to be there? Good question. For the moment, let's assume it was teleported there from the Starship Enterprise. We're trying to keep this simple.) So this cow appears, and then what happens? What do you actually have to do to avoid hitting the cow? You have to notice it and decide to hit the brake. You have to move your foot to the brake pedal and push. Your brakes have to first slow down the rate at which your wheels are spinning and finally stop them entirely. Throughout this wheel slowing process your tires have to maintain grip on the road surface. (If this part doesn't happen, if you're on glare ice, for example, none of the rest matters.)

At ten miles an hour, I suggested that there was plenty of time to avoid hitting the cow, but that's true only if all goes well and I count at least four variables here, four places where it could go wrong. First, you might not be paying perfect attention. How long does it take you to notice the cow once it has appeared? If you're looking down at your iPod when the cow appears, your reaction might be delayed by a second or so, possibly even more. Instead of 3.5 seconds to deal with the situation, you might have only 2.5. Next, how long does it take you to physically move your foot to the brake pedal in full on panic mode? Young people are physically quicker than older people, but practice also makes a slight difference since unfamiliar actions take longer than familiar ones. Third, how well do your brakes work? They are hopefully in good repair, but even if they are, some cars have better brakes than others. And finally, how well do your tires grip the road? Is the road wet or dry? What sort of tires do you have--soft sticky tires that wear out fast but really grab the pavement or nice hard tires that last forever but tend to slide around a bit? I had some sticky tires once on a Toyota Celica. I'd traded away a fine set of longer lasting Michelins to get them. And when the day came that a deer teleported itself into the roadway in front of me, it was the sticky tires that saved its life.

Now I have to tell you, most of the time, when an object appears suddenly on the road in front of you as if teleported there, it probably isn't really due to teleportation. It just seems that way because you have no idea how it actually got there because just a fraction of a second ago you didn't even know the cursed thing existed. I'm not going to say it's never teleportation, cuz how would I really know that for sure? But usually...usually it's not.

We have established, then, that speed is dangerous and that speed is a contributing factor in as many as 100% of all accidents involving moving vehicles. And now that we have done that, I know what some of you are saying. You're saying "Screw you, I'm going to go fast anyway." Well, of course you are. That's because you're an idiot. I may not know you well enough to know if you're one of the bigger idiots or one of lesser idiots, but still. I do recognize a fellow idiot when I hear one.

What we both recognize, of course, is that there's more to life than avoidance of risk, that safety is all very well but that safety is a negative virtue. Danger is a continuum; at one end are courses of action (or non-action) that are very, very safe and at the other end are actions that are very, very dangerous-- almost certain to cause harm to ourselves or to others. It's clearly no good trying to live your life at either extreme; you either end up quickly dead or you never really get to live. So the question is where on the continuum you want to be at any given moment. It's a pretty important question when you're driving a car and we should never forget it. But it's not the only question, far from it. What I think is that there is a certain perfect speed for every moment of driving. And since conditions can change from moment to moment, the perfect speed for a drive of any distance will be a series of variations in speed, each change being the exactly correct response to the conditions obtaining. Of course we hardly every get 'perfect' or 'exactly correct' but you know what I mean.

I think all good drivers know this, though they may not be conscious of it or may not express it in those terms. The thing I need to stress here is that when I say 'conditions obtaining' I am thinking about a whole raft of things. Road conditions are important. What kind of road is it? How heavy is the traffic? How fast are other people going? What is the weather like?

How's the visibility? What is the condition of the pavement? The condition of your car is important. How good are the brakes? Do your tires have any tread? And your condition is a factor. Are you relaxed? Are you angry? Do you have plenty of time to get where you're going? Or did you not allow enough time? What is your purpose in driving right now? Who is in the car with you? All of these things flow together to make you aware of just what the right speed is.

Now I'm not saying that we think all of this through consciously every moment we are driving. Not at all. I'm trying to say it consciously here, because words are what writers use. But the strange thing about driving is how wordless it is, how physical it is, how a car is a natural extension of our body, how driving becomes as instinctual as walking. People express dismay sometimes at the number of accidents that occur every year and the number of drivers and passengers who are injured or die, and of course these events are tragic. But have you ever had the experience of looking at it from the other perspective? I remember very well a moment long ago when I was driving on a busy four-lane thoroughfare. I suddenly saw it all of a piece, people making right turns, people stopped for left turns, lights alternating from red to green and back again, most drivers zipping along at 40 or 50 miles an hour, each driver guiding great masses of metal weighing well over a ton. It seemed like a flat out miracle that the system worked at all. Dozens of vehicles were flying by every minute and nobody ran into anyone! How could all these people--young and old, of all shapes and sizes and orientations, of all levels of education, to say nothing of variations in IQ, personal hygiene, political persuasion and general attitude toward life--how could they all manage to co-exist on this busy road without killing each other far more frequently than they actually do? That's when I started to realize that driving is natural to us.

Nature might not be the first thing you think of when you think about driving. Let's see...pick an image. How about a Cadillac Escalade pulling up to the entrance of an expensive hotel? Or a half dozen bunched up NASCAR race cars roaring past a grandstand full of 100,000 fans? How about an overhead shot of a complicated freeway interchange? Are we feeling natural yet? Maybe not, but maybe we should be. My feeling is that just like deer are really good at jumping and monkeys are really good at swinging from trees, humans are really good at driving. But it can't be natural, you might say, because it only got started about a hundred years ago and human beings have been around for thousands of years. It's an add on, it's artificial. Well, artificial as it may be, it also looks a lot like evolution, it looks like something that happened to grow naturally out of something that we already had in us. Yes, driving is learned; you're not born knowing how to do it. But you're not born knowing how to walk either. And yes, driving is different from walking in that there are some abstract rules and regulations that walking doesn't involve. But how else do you explain how we can manage to do this inherently dangerous thing so successfully? You have to admit we have a natural talent for it.

Want more proof? Think about all the bruhaha about driving while talking on your cell phone or while finishing your makeup or eating a sandwich or fiddling around with your car's sound system. Yes, these activities do increase the inherent dangerousness of driving. But the fact that people do this quite often and that most of them don't die or cause accidents is just further evidence that we're good at driving. We're so good we can do it with one hand tied behind our backs! We can do it and chew gum at the same time!

So part of the explanation for how we know exactly how fast we ought to go is that we just naturally do. We know it in our body; we know it in our reptilian brain; we know it from the sum total of our perceptions. The other part of the explanation lies the front brain, as indeed how could it not? Because, as we know, the front brain butts into pretty much everything. In the case of driving, it allows us to consciously decide how fast we want to go. More broadly, we can consciously decide what manner of driving we want to do. Let's imagine a hire car driver with two passengers who need to be transported to a place about 70 miles away. They have stated as part of the deal that they find riding in a car to be an unpleasant necessity and they expect the driver to minimize that unpleasantness. What is the perfect speed for the conditions obtaining here? The goal is to make the trip as quickly as possible so as to minimize the amount of time that the passengers must spend in the car, but also to make it as smooth and quiet as possible so as to minimize the level of discomfort that they feel. Whatever the traffic and road conditions might be, here's what we would have to suggest to the driver:

> Choose a very quiet, comfortable car
> Drive very slowly around curves and corners
> Drive quite fast on the straights, but only if you can...
> Accelerate and decelerate very slowly

Okay, now let's take something a little harder. Let's say you're a thirty-three year old driver who happens to be single and owns a sports car. You're going out on a date with someone you don't know well but who is about your age and to whom you are strongly attracted. Your outing involves driving to a place about 30 miles away. What is the perfect speed for this outing? Here are some questions you might ask yourself beforehand:

> Do I personally like to drive fast and take risks?
> If no, should I drive in my normal safe manner or should I drive faster and with a higher risk level than usual because I think it will impress my date?
> If yes, should I drive in my favorite fast, risky style or should I dial it down so as to avoid making myself look like an idiot?

Relationships are complicated and that this does not begin to exhaust the list of possible questions. What about the age of the driver? Would any of the answers be different if the age was twenty-three? Or forty-three? And I'll add one more thing. The smart driver in this situation will realize that having a particular individual in the seat next to you is just another part of the conditions that obtain. Conditions change from moment to moment. You can experiment a little and try to read your date's reactions. You might even ask. At some point your date might conceivably say "I totally hate going fast; if you have to do it, let me out of the car." That might not be the answer you wanted, but it's a helpful answer because you would then know that you were with someone who was totally confused about life and the nature of reality, possibly as a result of some previous trauma or flawed upbringing. A relationship with this person would mean taking on a project. On the other hand, the person might say "I like watching how people drive. It says something about them." Now that would be an answer! It doesn't solve any mysteries; it promises to keep them alive.

Ultimately, however, to get at this question of speed, we have to get everybody else out of the car. Sometimes having a passenger is just too complicated. So let's just say you're driving by yourself in your Jaguar, a car that is quite capable of going quite fast. And let's assume for a moment, just in a kind of a dream, that there are no other cars on the road, and that the road has a lot of variety in terms of ups and downs and straights and curves. I'm going to suggest that the perfect speed for this situation is pretty damn fast. Of course it depends on whether you're up for it. Driving fast is hard and the extra danger lends a certain tension to things. Sometimes you might not want that, you might want to drive just to relax. Maybe, but maybe not. Maybe the best way to 'relax' is to get very involved in something very different from the usual burdensome crap. And this thing you're going to get involved in is driving a car, and, as it turns out, the whole point of driving a car is to go fast. I've talked about how cars are magic. There is a thrill to speed that is akin to the idea of flying. The magic of cars is precisely that they extend our abilities; they allow us to go way faster and way farther than we could if we only relied on our own bones and muscles.

The question of how much faster is really pretty simple. It's not that there is any arbitrary logical limit, some fixed point at which you stop the magic and cut yourself off from whatever remaining magic might be left. Nobody goes out to get in their car and thinks "I could walk to work at 2.5 miles an hour, but my goal is to go exactly ten times that fast so I'll take the car and go 25 miles an hour. There's just no reason to go any faster." Oh no, that's not how it works. We want to go as fast as we reasonably can. We want it all, the whole magical enchilada, and that's as it should be.

It's not that the magic is limitless. It most definitely has a limit, the speed at which the magic fails and things go bad--either we hit somebody or we run off the road or we get stopped by the police. But we are fated to always be looking for that limit and to be desirous of approaching it. It's an entertaining quest for a number of reasons, not least of which is that the limit constantly changes according to the conditions that obtain. And to talk about that, let's get back to that open road with light traffic and no police. The limiting conditions here are the capabilities of the vehicle and how straight the road happens to be at any given point. If the road is straight and clear, we can just put our foot down and see how fast we can go. If the road curves, then things get a lot more complicated. But in either case, the capability of our car will be a critical factor.

A long straight will enable us to find our car's true top speed. This seems to me to be a perfectly natural thing to want to find out. And we will 'find' this speed in two senses. First, we will find out what it feels like to drive that car as fast as it will go. This is called having the real physical but superhuman experience. Second, we will find out what our speedometer reads when we do that. That's interesting too. It's kind of abstract--and it might not even be totally accurate because speedometers vary--but it's easy to explain and it gives us a number we can compare with other numbers. In practice, of course, we rarely drive for long at the top speed of our vehicles even if the road permits. That's partly because normal vehicles are rarely really happy at their maximums. That's why that old truck was complaining. It was most comfortable when it was not going absolutely as fast as it could go. I had a Miata once with a top speed of 110 or so. (It was a 1992 model.) I didn't drive it at 110 very often or for any length of time. There were a lot of reasons for that, but one was that the Miata wasn't very happy at speeds over 85. And by not happy I mean that the engine sounded and felt like it was working too hard. Throttle response was almost nonexistent. You had to just sit there on the gas while the speedometer needle crawled upward.

The Jaguar is both the same and different. It has a top speed of 155 mph. I've never driven it quite that fast and I expect that it wouldn't be happiest up there if I did, just like the Miata wasn't happy at its top speed. The difference, as you might imagine, is how the Jaguar feels a little lower down, say, in the area between 70 and 100. In that range the Miata is starting to flag, but the Jag is deep in the power band of the middle gears, the acceleration pressing you back against your seat and the speedometer needle shooting up the left side of the dial to the 90 mph mark at the top and then heading down the right side into the triple digits. In the Jaguar, 0 to 60 is fun, but so is 60 to 100. What a rush.

So, uh, if the Jaguar is so much faster than the Miata, why do so many people rave about Miatas, calling them some of the best cars of all time? Well, that's because going straight is only part of the speed story, and not necessarily the most interesting part. The other part has to do with going around curves. Turning is a lot harder than going straight and in practice a lot more dangerous. To run off the road when it is dry and straight, you have to be really careless. Basically you have to either fall asleep or have one of your front wheels fall off. On a curve though, all you have to do is make a small mistake, like turning the wheel either a little too much or not quite enough or simply just going a little too fast. And because it's more challenging and more involving than going straight, turning can be more rewarding.

Driving around a curve may not be as simple as driving in a straight line, but it's not all that complicated either. Basically, you just turn that round thing that your hands are on and, presto, the car starts to turn. But exactly how that happens, or more precisely, how the whole experience feels when it happens, that's one of the most fascinating things in all of driving. And the reason for this goes back to the magic, the beyond-human-ability aspect of driving. In a straight line the feelings of acceleration and of deceleration both give us those weird back brain thrills, but when we reach a simple, constant speed and just maintain it, the excitement is not so much. In that situation we tend to forget what speed is. But as soon as we turn, the forces of inertia start pushing us sideways, reminding us once again that we aren't just walking through the corn in Kansas anymore. There's a conflict between where our bodies and organs naturally want to go (straight ahead) and where the car is taking us. Suddenly the body is reminded that we're actually traveling at a magical 20 or 30 or 130 miles an hour, and it tends to wake right up.

I should mention here that one of the interesting things about turning is that we don't really have to feel that conflict if we don't want to. Remember that example about the hire car and the two passengers who found driving unpleasant? It sounded as if the driver was in for sort of a boring ride. But not entirely. There is a sort of driving, usually when the driver has multiple passengers, where minimizing the sense of motion is a worthy goal--and to make it interesting, all we have to do is add one more idea: at the same time you try to minimize the sense of motion, try to go as fast as possible. Now to do that, you absolutely can't go around sharp corners very fast, you can't brake too hard and you can't accelerate hard. But still, but still. There are things you can do. Try them sometime. But I digress.

As I said back in Chapter 1, some people want to notice what's happening as they drive and negotiating a curve at a reasonably high speed is a great place for doing that. Cars are different in how they respond to that situation. Some cars wallow, which is to say that they exhibit body roll. While the four wheels and the chassis stay flat on the ground, the body of the car, which of course includes the passenger compartment, tilts sideways like an ocean liner rolling in a swell. I was once a passenger in an early fifties Plymouth, driven by a fellow who was not in a particularly good mood. He needed to turn left off of a highway and onto a side road, but he came upon the side road sooner than he expected. (And that had something to do with his mood and life circumstances at that time, or so I speculate.) He didn't have time to slow down, but he turned anyway. Suddenly the world went all diagonal on us for a bit as the body rolled right and the wheels pulled left. We all looked for something to grab onto as we slid sideways and down across the bench seats. The car did not turn over and in a moment it righted itself and all was calm once again.

Body roll is exciting, but most people find it unpleasant and carmakers try to minimize it, especially in sports cars. Another time, I was in the back of a Mazda RX-7 whose driver was in quite a good mood but who made a similar sharp fast turn. We were driving in a residential area, looking for a particular street onto which we needed to make a right turn. As we approached one particular street, my girlfriend at the time, who was occupying the other front seat and who was also in a fine mood, was navigating. She was saying something like "Hmm. I don't think it's this one...uh...no wait, it **is** this one." Now by the time she said that we were most of the way through the intersection, but, since this was the one, the driver whipped the wheel to the right and down that street we went. Despite the violence of the maneuver, the car stayed flat with hardly a trace of body roll. Nice car, the RX-7. But you may remember I said that I was in the back of the car. Did you think I was in a seat? There are no seats in the back of an RX-7, no place to sit up, just a bit of space between the roof and an uneven expanse of hard black plastic that a 'passenger' has to sort of lie down and scrunch up on. There's nothing to grab onto either, so when the car turns hard to the right, such a passenger just naturally slams up against the wall on the left. And do you get any sympathy from the occupants of the two comfortably bolstered front seats when this happens? Might one's possible injuries be cause for concern? Not in my case. If anything, the two in front went on in an even better mood than before.

So all cars turn and all cars can turn sharply, maybe too sharply for conditions. How they do so is really quite endlessly interesting. We've seen that some cars show lots of body roll and others less. We can also describe cars as turning lightly or heavily, accurately or sloppily, instantly or hesitantly, and--I don't know--probably lots of other words too. In any case, these turning or cornering qualities don't show themselves much when cars turn while moving slowly. It takes speed to make them noticeable. And guess what? The more speed you have the more noticeable they are. At very high speeds relative to the sharpness of the curve, a turning car's tires will lose grip and start to slide. What an interesting development that is! Interesting because if it's not too serious you have this nice sensation of first losing control but then regaining it and also interesting because if it is too serious you run off the road and possibly die. You can't get much more interesting than that.

Another interesting thing is that cars lose grip in different ways. In most cars the front tires lose grip first. Let's say you've turned your wheel to the right to go around a curve but you're going a little too fast. The car will start to turn right, but then if the front tires start to slide a bit, you find that the car is not turning nearly as much as you told it to. To some extent it's still going straight ahead, which is a pretty bad thing. In other cars the rear wheels start sliding first, especially if the driver is trying to accelerate. In this case when you turn the wheel to the right, the car starts to go that way just as in the first case. But then the rear wheels lose grip and the back of the car swings out to the left. You find that the car has rotated too much and you're now sideways in the road, which is not a good thing either. The reason people rave about Miatas is that they are balanced and tend not to understeer (front slippage) or oversteer (rear slippage). Instead, if you go too fast around a curve, all four wheels lose grip at the same time, the entire car leaps off the road, and you die.

Well, not really, just a little Jaguar owner humor there. Ha-ha. Poor Miata driver. DOA. Hilarious. Okay, I'm sorry. It's just that I'm a little jealous. People go on and on about Miatas. Isn't anyone ever going to claim that the 1996-2006 generation of XK Jaguars are among the greatest cars ever made? Sigh. In fact, Miatas **are** balanced, and if you go very fast they will sometimes lose grip in both the front and the rear at once, but this happens gradually and unless you're going ridiculously

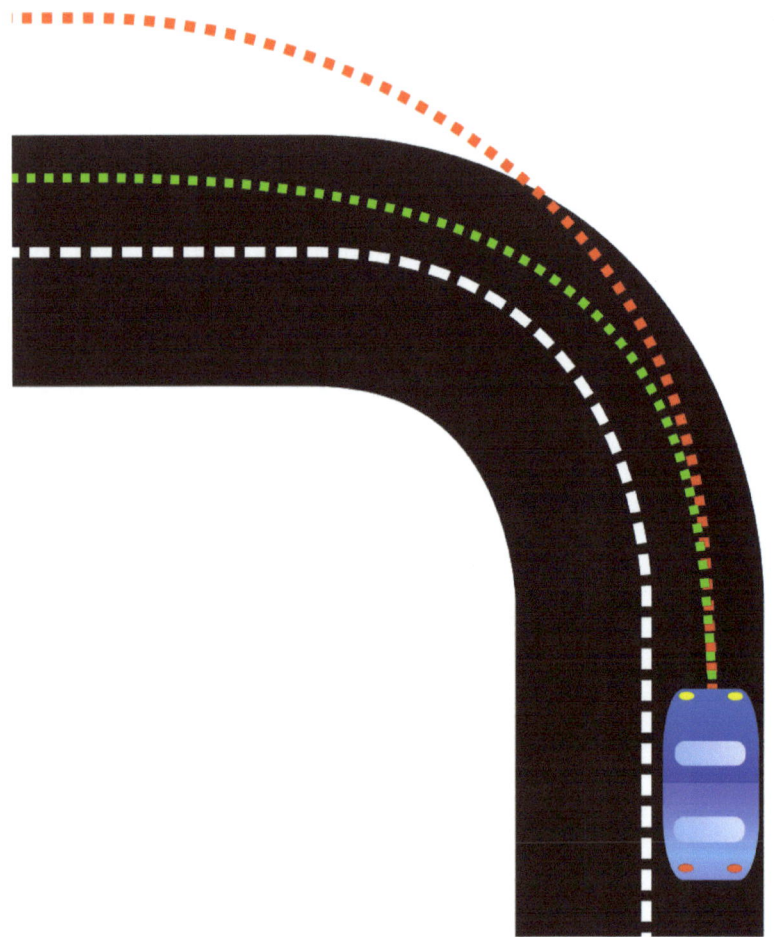

A basic depiction of understeer. At low speeds you turn the steering wheel just enough so as to follow the road; your course is the dotted green line. At some higher speed you turn the steering wheel that same amount to follow that same course, but the front tires slide forward instead of going to the left and the car follows the dotted red line. The solution is to turn the wheels even more, just as the driver in the top photo on the next page has done. This won't help, however, if you're going really fast, so slowing down might also be a good idea, especially if there are large trees or steep cliffs in the area.

Speed

You can't see understeer in a still photo, but that's probably what's happening here. The driver is turning the wheels sharply to the right, but not because she wants to drive into the circle. Instead, she is going fast enough that the front tires are slipping and she has to compensate merely to continue going around the circle. If we had a video of this, we could more easily see that the car was not turning to the right nearly as much as it ought to be given the angle of the front wheels.

This Mercedes has lost rear wheel grip on this wet surface as the driver negotiates a right hand curve. The rear end of the car has swung out to the left . This is oversteer. Notice the angle of the front tires. They are turned slightly to the left even though this is a right hand turn. This is how good drivers react to oversteer. In a moment the rear of the car will stop sliding and the driver will begin changing the wheel angle back to normal right turn mode.

fast, the Miata is naturally able to compose itself just enough so that you can step along through the curve without the ugliness of pushing your nose or sliding your tail. It just works. People like Miatas because the words that describe how they turn are words like accurate, light, nimble and responsive. And that's exactly how they make the driver feel--provided the driver is paying attention.

And so what about the Jaguar XKR, a car that weighs almost twice as much as a Miata? What happens if you go around a curve fast in that? Well, as we saw in Chapter 1, the words to describe the Jag's behavior are not 'light' or 'nimble' or 'quick'. But 'heavy' or 'hesitant' or 'slow' aren't right either. We'll try and find some right words later. For the moment, we'll just note that going around curves in a Jaguar, not too fast but fast enough to push you hard up against the side bolsters in your seat, well...that is a very fine thing to do. I recommend it to anyone.

In these last few paragraphs I have separated straight lines from curves, so as to do each one justice. All well and good, but now let's put them back together. Let's try to see that they are all part of the one experience; neither exists without the other. And that notion is part of a greater topic than mere speed and so we must save it for the chapter on Driving a Jaguar Properly and bring this chapter to a close

No discussion of speed would be complete, however, without a mention of speed limits. Few of us spend our driving lives solely on racetracks or autobahns where we are free to go as fast as we like. The roads we drive on have rules about speed and we can be punished if we break them. There are two aspects to the speed limit industry. First, there is one whole set of bureaucrats and engineers in charge of setting the limits. They have been working on this for a long time and have pretty much managed to set a speed limit for every single road just about everywhere in the world, the only exceptions being a few roads in Germany and on the Isle of Man. We often wonder about these people, especially when the posted limit seems too low. In Oregon the maximum limits are 65 on the freeway and 55 everywhere else. These limits are a bit lower than the national average, but lots of states are similar. I have to say, though, that in Oregon just about everyone exceeds the speed limit. In fact the vast majority of drivers in the US routinely exceed the speed limit. More about that later. Texas and Utah have the highest limits. Both have a limit of 80 on most freeways and Texas has one stretch of road where the limit is 85.

Besides the people who set the limits, there's another group of people who are charged with enforcing them and these are of course our city, county and state police. For city and county officers, speed enforcement is just one of many, many things they have to do, and maybe not one of the most important ones. State patrol officers specialize more in speed enforcement, but even they have other duties. Enforcement is problematic. Strict, continuous enforcement is expensive in terms of labor and equipment costs and is not really cost effective. There's a big revenue spike when such a program starts, but once it's been going on for a while the local drivers adjust and revenue falls. Another problematic aspect is that almost all drivers exceed the speed limit in practice, though not by much. Thus the limits are in fact guidelines. Few officers will ticket drivers for exceeding the speed limit by 5 mph, or even 10. Left to their own devices, police officers will be looking for more serious violations, drivers who are trying to go much faster than the regular flow of traffic, people who are doing things like weaving in and out and driving on the shoulder and generally acting stupid. We must note, regretfully, that officers are not always left to use their own judgment in this area. Instead, they may be heavily incentivized to issue lots of tickets. Since studies show that a high percentage of drivers are exceeding the limit at any given time, an ambitious officer will almost certainly be able to meet his or her quota. The main result, though, is not justice or increased safety; it is more of a particularly random and capricious form of taxation.

I hope that I have sufficiently established--in my Starship Enterprise cow example--that the dangerousness of driving increases as speed rises. But I have also suggested that the right speed depends on conditions. Almost everyone driving on

I-5 in Oregon goes faster than the speed limit. That's partly because they know that the probability of a cow being teleported onto the highway 50 feet in front of them is really low. In fact, it is safe to say that although cows once in great while get through onto a freeway in Oregon, your chances of colliding with one are infinitesimal. That's the most salient feature of dual carriageway roads. The people who built them have gone to great lengths to make them safe and they've done a pretty good job. Drivers know this, of course. It's obvious. It becomes part of the conditions of driving and the result is that people tend to go quite fast, not because they are raving maniacs who want to die but because they can see how much safer it is to go fast on the freeway than on most other sorts of roads.

The thing to remember is that the speed at which traffic naturally flows, even if it is 5, 10, 15, or 20 mph higher than the posted limit, is almost certainly a relatively safe speed. It is determined by how the drivers read the road conditions, and as mentioned, humans are really pretty good at this driving thing. Most of them actually do know, at any given moment, what's really dangerous and what isn't and they avoid the dangerous stuff. (Yes, there are exceptions; some young people, some drunk people, some drunk young people, a few people who go really, really fast in dense fog, etc. But the exceptions prove the rule.) One way to look at a busy freeway is to imagine that all or most drivers are insane, self-destructive, or stupid and that the only things preventing mass carnage are the posted limits and the brave police officers who enforce them. But this is delusional. Yes, there are some insane, self-destructive or stupid drivers and to the extent that their danger to others can be minimized, speed limits and speed enforcement might be good. (And we would do well to be thankful to have brave policemen to deal with them.)

But it is false to think that most drivers are like that and it is false to think that without posted limits all would devolve into chaos. And yet, this seems to be the model that we often use to make decisions about our highways. Sigh.

Chap 7: Approval

It's not hard to find glowing descriptions of Jaguars. People who own Jaguars like to talk about them, usually in very positive terms. The comments or user review sections of web sites are full of comments like "Fantastic car. I used to have an Accuporschillac. This Jaguar is so much finer!" or "By far the best car I've ever had." or "Always dependable if properly maintained." And then there are automobile publications and websites that provide professional quality approval, usually describing the Jaguar driving experience as exciting and pleasurable. Even when they criticize some aspects of particular Jaguar models, they are careful to also praise all the remaining aspects. So, you might think that buying a Jaguar is a no-brainer. Everyone should do it. Except of course that the foregoing sentences would also apply even if you took out the word "Jaguar" and substituted "Mercedes" or "Lexus" or "Honda" or "Hyundai" or just about any brand of automobile. In the first place, we know that car owners are not to be trusted; they're invested! There is nothing more natural for car lovers than to be in love with the car that they currently own.

And secondly, professional reviewers are also suspect. They all may appear to earn their money by providing an expert evaluation of a car based on a series of objective criteria. But is that really what they do? Well...sort of, but only within the basic parameters of their job, which are, on the one hand, to please their bosses by encouraging site hits or print subscriptions, and on the other, to please advertisers by making new cars sound so wonderful that readers are just going to have to go out and buy one. For the sake of credibility, they usually make some effort to appear objective, but true objectivity is problematic for any professional writer in that it does not automatically guarantee an adequate income. When it comes to making money, figuring out what others want to hear and then telling them that is a much safer bet.

The two most famous automotive media outlets in English are the Car Talk radio program in the U.S. (now defunct) and the BBC TV program Top Gear in the UK. How about getting some approval from one of those? That would be excellent. Let's say that one of those two were to announce that the 2004 XKR was a fantastic car. If that happened, my personal choice of car would be validated by a famous expert! Millions of listeners or viewers would also become potential approvers of my car! Wow. For someone who cared about such things, that would be great. So first, let's look at Car Talk. If you searched hard enough, you might be able to find their comments on the 2001 XK8 and XKR. But if you know Tom and Ray well, you won't even need to do that. You can predict what they'll have to say--and it will be mostly negative. They'll criticize the car for being rear wheel drive, based on the fact, presumably, that front wheel drive is more space efficient. They criticize it for being unsafe because it has too much power and goes too fast. They'll mock the ridiculous and unusable rear seats and they'll complain that the ride isn't soft enough. Other, less sporty Jaguars will do a little better in their eyes; they'll be praised for being quiet and comfortable with a smooth ride, but this will be faint praise of the damning variety.

The Car Talk guys are good on safety and functionality and on being sensible. They don't mind a little fun, but the Miata is as far as they'll go. It's so reliable, they might be thinking, and so not very fast. Once a woman called in and told them that her husband was thinking of adding a supercharger to their Miata. They were aghast. Don't let him do it, they said, unless you really don't like him and you're hoping he'll kill himself. ("You'll shoot your eye out!") So for Jaguar owners looking for approval, assuming such people exist, there's not much to be found at Car Talk, especially if the Jaguar in question is an XKR. In fact, if I were an author given to quoting the experts, I could

Approval

have quoted Tom and Ray in the Chapter 1 of this book. They'd contribute their own reasons why you're glad you don't own my car.

So what about Top Gear? Sigh. Top Gear loves Jaguars, raves about them, and has even been known to claim that they're better than Porsches, Mercedes or even Aston Martins. The question, though, is whether you're going to be able to take any of it seriously. Top Gear raves about all sorts of things, and finds a new fantastic, unbeatable car every week. Jaguars will be raved about when their turn comes up, but so will a host of other cars. A little later I'll talk about what it means if your car meets with the approval of an eleven-year-old. Here, we have to consider what it means if your car meets with the approval of...well, of what exactly? Top Gear is brilliant in its way, but any opinions expressed are mostly for effect. Sincerity, though it seems to pop up now and again, is definitely not the dominant mode. The show is a form of reality TV; its road tests and other features are scripted for drama and entertainment value and its three stars are all reasonably good actors. They are meant to be ordinary guys, but they come off as the sort of ordinary guys who are desperate for attention, alternately attractive and repellent. Jeremy Clarkson leads the way and plays a role almost as old as theatre, a modernized version of the blustery Miles Gloriosus character as created by Plautus in 200 B.C. Top Gear at its best is good entertainment, as good as Plautus anyway. But it is not by any stretch reliable.

In 2008 the top gear presenters made fun of the Tesla and were later sued by Tesla for libel. Although it seemed clear that the presenters had made at least one negative statement about the car that they knew to be inaccurate, the court dismissed the libel suit on the basis that Top Gear's purpose is to entertain and not to inform. Well, okay, but does everyone who watches the show understand that it's really just pretend? The Tesla is an American car and America bashing is another ingredient in the Top Gear recipe. In fact there's a hefty dollop of pro-British chauvinism throughout. Although Jaguar has been foreign owned since 1992, the company retains some plausible Britishness and of course it serves Top Gear's purposes to focus on that and ignore the ownership question as much as possible. Add it all up and you're guaranteed to get rabid approval of Jaguars, at least from time to time, and it's not entirely bogus either. We just have to take it with a small iceberg of salt.

Outside the big two, most mass media reviews, articles and video segments about Jaguar pronounce some variation of the same basic message: "Jaguars are not quite as good technically as Mercedes or BMWs but they are still beautiful and desirable cars that offer a special driving experience." The trick here is to help meet the sales targets of Jaguar executives and soothe the egos of Jaguar owners while at the same time providing comfort to Mercedes and BMW executives and flattery for Mercedes and BMW owners, who vastly outnumber Jaguar owners in the reading or viewing audience.

So if I really want to know what others think about my Jaguar, who should I listen to? Who can I trust? How do I get approval? Now I am tempted to say that the correct answers to these three questions are: "Listen to no one", "Trust no one" and "You can't", but that would be boring. Besides, it's not that simple. No matter how tough we are, approval is nice. It's one of those basic human needs. Many people actually long for approval. (I know you're not like that and I'm not either, but, really, many people are.) I have a 1989 Toyota Corolla and in 2010, when it was twenty-one years old, I had it painted. It wasn't a premium paint job, but it was a pretty good one and it cost me $800. It was a fairly low mileage car--just 55,000 back then--and that's one of the factors that I used to justify this expense. I had to justify it somehow, because strictly on financial grounds it didn't work out. Basically, I was spending $800 on a car that was only worth $1,000, or with a new paint job, maybe $1,100. My sister did not approve; she thought it was a foolish and frivolous expense. My wife approved; she was embarrassed to be seen in it with the paint the way it was. My mother was stuck in the middle. We talked about it a little, but she never said what she thought. If I were someone who cared about others' approval, which of course I am not, I might think that actually she did sort of approve, she just didn't want

Approval

to say so.

We have to face the fact that some people--let's call them practical people-- will never approve of buying a Jaguar. They'll lean toward the Car Talk view. They'll say it's too fast and too fancy and a waste of money. Some of those same people will be a little more likely to approve of a Cadillac or a Mercedes. Even though these cars are also fast and fancy and expensive, people might just say "Well, it's a lot of money, but they're nice cars and he/she/they can afford it, so why not?" And what if the car is a Porsche or a Ferrari? In that case, if the driver is a young person, people will say "That's a terrible idea. They're going to kill themselves in that car." If it's an older person, such people will just say "midlife crisis" and dismiss the whole thing as foolishness, usually male foolishness. And speaking of which, have you noticed that BMW Z-4 drivers are much more likely to be females than Porsche Boxster drivers? Why is that exactly? But I digress. Practical people only approve of practical cars, preferably small electric ones, and some people don't approve of any cars at all. We can't expect much from them.

It used to be that if you had a nice car, especially a convertible, and you really needed approval, all you had to do was find some young people between the ages of seven and seventeen. These tweens and teens--especially but not exclusively the males--could be counted on to stare admiringly at your car and the bolder of them would say complimentary things. Sadly, this doesn't happen so much anymore. There are still a few young people for whom cars are a fascination, but the golden age of young people dreaming of cars has passed, at least in the United States. Of course this automotive adoration from young people was always problematic. It's great to have an eleven-year-old admire your car, but how much does an eleven-year-old really know about anything? Hmm. You will notice that the way I have put that question makes it sound rhetorical, the obvious answer being "Not much." But lest we be too dismissive of the opinions of eleven-year-olds, keep in mind that the question could be rephrased as "How much of what an eleven-year-old instinctively intuits about the world have we lost by the time we're twenty?" That's a pretty complex question and I won't try to answer it, but I think it's just possible that in true fullness of understanding, having children admire your car is actually pretty cool and might be one of the best and truest forms of approval that you're ever likely to get. Still, for children to admire your car, first they have to notice it and these days not too many will.

So what about approval from grown-up children, one's own children perhaps? In the middle class world, such as it is, folks who buy nice cars tend to be older people who can afford it because their children are out of the house and out of college and doing okay on their own. That describes me, for example, sort of. So if, after a life of minivans and Volvos, you are thinking of buying a very different kind of car like, say, a Jaguar, you're going to wonder if your children will approve. Will they think less of you? If it's one of the higher priced Jags, will they be disgusted and disappointed that you are not managing your resources more effectively so as to maximize their inheritance? More importantly, will they be disgusted and disappointed at such selfish and childish behavior from someone they used to look up to? Looking around at the grown children I know, I suspect that the answers to both these questions will usually be negative and that the kids will actually think it's kind of neat to see the old folks having some fun. But, on the other hand, if the children do have serious concerns in these areas, parents will owe them an explanation. Such an explanation might run something like this: "I know that you disapprove of me making this decision and I know roughly why you disapprove; you disapprove partly because that is how I raised you. I may in fact have taught you that you were supposed to disapprove of decisions like this. Which seemed like a good idea to me at the time. But this is a new time and at this particular time, I am buying a Jaguar. Deal with it."

Children, then, yours or someone else's, may or may not be good sources of approval. Siblings, parents and spouses should be good sources, but there are all sorts of possible family dynamics that might get in the way. Other Jaguar owners are biased, and professional auto writers are not necessarily to be trusted. If we reject all of these, we have just one group left to turn to: total strangers--people who don't own Jaguars, don't write about cars for a living, and don't know you from Adam. Let's see what they have to say about my car. (We'll just use me as an example; as mentioned above, we know that I am not really seeking for anyone's approval about anything. Any more than you are.) Here are some unsolicited comments that have been made about my 2004 XKR:

"That's a really beautiful color with the sun shining on it." --gas station attendant

"That's a beautiful car." --gate monitor at a car show

Beautiful car! And thanks for bringing it with the top down." --another gate monitor at the same car show.

"Nice car!" --station attendant

"That's about ten kinds of perfect. Want to trade keys?" --gas station attendant

"Who gave you permission to drive my car?" --man with two grandchildren in tow in a supermarket parking lot

"That must be a lot of fun to drive." --man with a shaved head and a PhD

"That's a gorgeous car. You must have a lot of fun in that." --woman in the adjacent parking space downtown

"That's a beautiful color." --man who just got out of another Jaguar convertible, a candy apple red XJS.

What a discerning and cultured group of people! And to think I ran into them more or less at random over the course of just a few months. Amazing. Now it's possible that some of these comments may strike you as unsophisticated. You might think that the speakers may be responding to mere outward appearance, either commenting on appearance directly or else using appearance to make dubiously valid inferences about the driving experience. Well that's fine with me. Either way, they're saying that there's something to admire about the car, something desirable. They might be responding to the car the way an eleven-year-old would--only they're not eleven. This has to be good.

 The speakers were a somewhat varied group in terms of age and circumstance; all we know for sure about them is that they noticed the car and chose to express a positive opinion of it. The rest of the world either hasn't noticed my car or hasn't chosen to speak about it. That seems to be the way it is. There is one group of people in the world who tend to notice and care about cars. I've always been one of them. There is another group who don't notice cars and couldn't care less about them. If a person were looking for approval--which of course you and I are not--we wouldn't get much from this second group. Even if they were polite and said something nice, we'd see it for what it was. So thank goodness for the first group. And also for the third group, maybe the largest. These are the people in the middle, people who don't notice cars often but who are not unaware of their importance and who do tend to notice certain cars on certain occasions. People in this group may not give much thought to the cars they drive today and yet if they think back, they may still recall another car that they were particularly fond of at some earlier time of life. These people are at least moderately sane. Which reminds me, is affection for a car somehow connected to youth? Youth, as you may remember if you're older and as I hope you are realizing if you are young, is a time of freedom, a time of infinite possibility spreading out before us as well as a time of effortless physical motion. As many have noted, it is wasted on the young. But I digress.

 The last quote on my list, as you may have noticed, is from another Jaguar owner, and that brings up the question of what kind of approval you can get from that category of people. I've suggested at the beginning of this chapter that they are likely to be less than reliable sources because they are generally biased in favor of Jaguars, but that's both simplistic and not really fair. You could just as easily say that Jaguar owners are exactly the people you do want approval from, because they are the experts. The fact that they have Jaguars of their own proves that they are intelligent, discerning, and knowledgeable people. Now at this point, off in the distance, you might hear the faint sound of a Mercedes owner (or some other very confused person) saying "No, it proves that they are fools." You can ignore that sound.

Actually most Jaguar owners are indeed quite knowledgeable and aware. They tend to speak very highly of the experience of driving their cars; they love the comfort, the looks and the performance. They know the difference between sports cars and grand tourers and they don't criticize their cars for not being Porsches. They are usually less happy about the cost and frequency of repairs. A typical comment about older, pre-Ford era Jags goes something like this: "High maintenance and shocking cost to repair, but still great value for money." I'm not sure that is a completely rational statement, but never mind. Owners of later Jaguars--like mine--report fewer repair problems, but still say things like "Expensive car to run, but worth every penny." This is better, subjective perhaps but not insane. It's basically my attitude, though I must say that the pennies are mounting up.

A few months ago I decided to try and get a little more insight into the Jaguar world by joining a Jaguar owners club. I then entered my car in a car show and spent a day getting broiled in the sun looking at few hundred mostly older British cars and voting for which ones I liked best in each of a mind-numbing number of categories. My car didn't win any prizes at the show but it did get a fair amount of attention. Guys tended to stand around looking at it, maybe a bit more than most of the other cars in my category. I'll take that as approval. It was hard, though, because to tell you the truth my category--Jags less than twenty years old--was one of the most boring categories in the show. A lot more attention went to the E-

Types from the sixties and seventies and to the XK120/140/150 family of cars from the fifties. Plus there was an even earlier car, a very beautiful pearl white Jaguar saloon. I think it was a so-called Mark IV, a model that was first produced in 1936 and later re-launched after the war, being replaced in 1949 by the Mark V. I first saw this particular car on a trailer in a motel parking lot the night before the show. On the day of the show it was parked off by itself. It had no competitors in its class.

There were plenty of competitors in the other classes though and competition was pretty keen. The car that took first place in my category was a 2007 car that looked showroom new. My wife and I spoke briefly to the owner, a friendly enough fellow, but pretty focused, maybe a little obsessive, definitely more of a laser than a lava lamp. Afterward, Eve and I were both thinking along the lines of retired surgeon. On his car, clearly, flaws are just not permitted; intervention follows immediately upon diagnosis. It's easy to imagine that the upper ranks of car show winners might be full of guys like this. It takes both money and serious attention to play. At any officially sanctioned Jaguar event, a distinction is made between the 'concours' category and the 'driven' category. This sounds pretty reasonable. Perfect show cars just can't be driven. If they were driven in the real world, their perfection wouldn't last. So they ride in trailers to and from the show. The concours class is for these jewel-like cars, the cars whose whole point is just to be beautiful and collectable. And they are indeed beautiful, combining an original beauty of design with the beauty of fine craftsmanship in the process of their restoration. Generally the cars with the newest and most ambitious restorations are the winners.

But we all know that there's something weird about cars that you can't drive around in. Cars that aren't driven aren't exactly cars. Hence, car shows also include the driven class, where the standards of beauty aren't quite so high and where in theory some wear and tear is expected. And this is a great category. There was an old Jaguar XJS convertible at the show that still had its original 30-year-old upholstery. The leather

Above: Jaguar XK 140, produced from 1954 to 1957
Below: Jaguar XK 150. produced from 1957 to 1961

In 1948, Jaguar claimed that the newly introduced XK120 would go 120 mph. Independent testing proved that it could. Were the later cars capable of 140 and 150 respectively? No. Both the 140 and 150 had top speeds around 130 mph.

1948 Jaguar Mark IV at the All British Field Meet in 2013. Internet prices for these cars range from c. $17,000 for a "good candidate for restoration" to c. $65,000 for a restored example. The most expensive one on offer as I write this is in Holland. They're asking 159,000 euros, but I bet they'd dicker.

There were plenty of early Triumphs at the show. My first British car was a TR3. It had been re-sprayed in dark blue metallic. It was way prettier than any of these--or so my memory claims.

was intact but it was dried and cracked everywhere and looked every year of its age. It was also quite beautiful, much more beautiful than new leather would have been, no matter how carefully the replacement might have been done. I had to vote that car number one in its category just for that reason. (I should explain here that I was voting in yet a third category: the "People's Choice." The concours and driven categories were both judged by small panels of connoisseurs.)

Alas, this great idea, this separation of trailer queens and driven cars into two categories is a situation ripe for gamesmanship. If you've been around the block at all, you can imagine what happens. Several people at the show were talking about cars that looked perfect enough for the concours class but were entered in the driven class. Driven they may have been, but probably not actually very darn much. Someone was looking for an easy win.

So...if you're thinking about getting approval for your car from a car show...well, it's a tricky business. Some people will approve of your car's brand but look down on you for having the wrong model, or for having little chips in your paint, or just for having a car that's not old enough. In general, in the Jaguar world, older cars are way cooler. This puts me in a difficult position; my car is old enough that it lacks the latest technology and the higher output of the new models, but it's too new to be really cool. It would be hard for me to win much approval even if I fixed some of its many gross imperfections. My car wants to turn into a show ready collector car, but it's too young and I'm not quite going for it. So if I need approval, I'm going to have to depend--like poor Blanche Dubois--on the kindness of strangers.

Chapter 8: Destinations

Sometimes when I go out and get into my car, I don't actually know where I'm going. I just feel like going for a drive. Of course I have to go somewhere; I just haven't decided where. First I've got to get the car out of the garage. That doesn't require any decision-making, but it does require care because the garage door opening isn't very much wider than the car. Once the car clears the garage, I have a turnaround space that I back into, again being very careful because I don't want to hit the stone retaining wall that sticks up about four feet on two sides of it. In a reasonable world garage openings would be wider and retaining walls--if they had to be there at all--would be made of foam rubber, but I digress.

After I finish backing up, not too far but far enough, I turn sharply left and go forward up thirty feet of driveway to the road. Now I have two problems. I have to be careful that no cars are coming from either direction and I have to decide which direction I'm going to go. But this decision actually doesn't mean much. The road I live on is a partial loop with just two outlets, and both of them lead out to the same feeder road. So this first decision doesn't matter a great deal. But when I do get down to that slightly larger road I come to a T junction. I can't go straight; I have to go left or right and its a momentous decision. It's like the whole continent splits into two vast areas.

If I turn right, I'll be headed basically south toward the nearest town, which happens to be on a major east-west route. Once I got to town I could go left across the valley and up into the Cascade mountains or I could go west over to the Pacific coast. Or I could just keep going south, to the town of Rice Hill, for example, which sits in a little valley and has a good ice cream place. If I kept on going I could reach Mount Shasta, or Sacramento, or Mexico City. But wait a minute, that might be a little far, for just going out on a drive. Anyway, that's all just if I turn right out of my little street. If I turn left, the road will lead me north, or at least northish, toward Portland, maybe through the vineyard country around Dundee, maybe all the way to Seattle, or Anchorage. What to do. What to do.

To keep things simple, let's say this excursion is limited to just a few hours, a sort of home before dinner thing, or a least home before bed. In that case it's not really the whole continent spread out before me in two giant halves. It's more like four or five counties. And since the point of all this is just to drive, you might say that the destination is unimportant, that there should be no destination, that the journey is all. Well that's all very fine, but I still have to decide whether to turn left or right onto that street that leads out of my neighborhood. When we do this kind of driving, it's natural to have a destination in mind, a destination that guides you in making those first turns out of your neighborhood and sets you on your way. What should this destination be? How about a vineyard? How about a little restaurant on the waterfront? How about just a view point in the mountains or a picnic in a campground? How about an antique shop or an outlet mall? That would be okay. On my last little drive I stopped at a Safeway and bought a loaf of bread and twenty-four ounces of ground coffee. That was okay too. There's nothing wrong with any of these places, but they're incidentals, pleasant encounters. They're just places. My real destination is almost always a road.

Or more exactly some stretch of road, or some sequence of roads, somewhere within the area of my reach. It may be a known and favorite road, it may be an unknown road I would like to explore. That's what I look forward to; that's what I plan around. I'm looking forward to the experience of the movement, not to the moment of arrival. Is it just me or are most people like that? I don't know for sure. It's possible that my priorities are skewed, at least as compared to the general population. Hello, my name is Michael, and I'm not going anywhere.

What kind of road am I looking for? Well, you can probably guess. It would be a road with not too much traffic and a rich variety of ups and downs and straights and curves. It would be a road where you can go somewhat fast. You'll remember from the speed chapter that I believe that every little piece of road has its right and perfect speed and that that speed is maybe a little faster than some people realize. Stop signs are okay in limited quantities; traffic lights are less acceptable. I'm looking for a road where I can go that speed, or something close to it, in a reasonably safe manner that involves no physical contact with animals either wild or domestic, no physical contact with other cars, and actually no physical contact with any other object at all except the road itself. Additionally I demand a low likelihood of law enforcement interest in my driving. Picky. Picky.

In the place where I grew up there weren't very many roads that would meet these criteria, at least not nearby. To the west of town there were lots of farm roads out in the flats. They met the criteria of not much traffic and not much speed enforcement, so yes a person could go fast there. In fact my earliest memory of speed was riding with my stepfather and his buddy in his buddy's pickup, a newish rig with a big V-8. He'd blast around out there at ninety miles an hour talking about the John Birch Society. But those roads were so straight and flat that they weren't all that interesting. On the other side of town, to the east, were the Wasatch Mountains and the only roads there were the highways that wound up through the canyons. Some of these were potentially interesting roads, but they all had heavy use and radar enforcement.

Where I live now is a different kind of place. The middle of the Willamette Valley is wide and flat, but along the edges there are miles and miles of foothills and smaller river valleys. There are dozens of roads winding through a mixture of low elevation forest and rolling hill farmland. Of course these aren't superfast roads. The Jaguar's top speed is 155 mph, so they say, and there aren't any places in these hills where you'd want to go that fast, not even close. But this part of Oregon is still a great place for driving; that's one reason I got stuck living here. There's a great mixture of tight curves and sweepers. The straights are not too long, but they're long enough. Pretty much nobody keeps it to fifty-five. In the forest parts the curves are blind and that's not so good; you don't know what you'll find. You have to cross your fingers a little to go fast around those. Mostly you worry about hitting a deer.

And then there's the traffic. For one thing, there are log trucks to contend with. They're big and ungainly and you might think they'd be slow. Think again. Farm machinery appears occasionally--sprayers or discs or combines--and they are really slow, of course, and tend to be on the wide side, sometimes too wide to even pass. That's a test of patience and a chance to look more carefully at the scenery. At certain times of the day there are middle-aged sedans and compacts that seem to belong to people who live out there. Some you pass and some you don't. Mostly they're moving right along, at least on straights. Once in a while you'll go to pass a slower car and the other driver will floor it trying to make things challenging for you. I love that because it gives me a chance to floor the Jag, which I don't normally do.

Thankfully, you don't see much in the way of minivans on these roads, but there are some old work trucks that just can't go fast and also some newish but oddly slow pickups with writing on the side that might mosey along well under the speed limit. You sometimes think that maybe the driver is working for someone else and getting paid by the hour. You have to pass them. It's easy and fun. The perfect road does not involve the total absence of traffic or the total absence of any stress or tension.

Occasionally I run across another fairly fast car out in the sticks and that creates a little tension. Is the other driver

Speed is neither a challenge nor a provocation. It is not a test...

and it has no meaning. It is a surge of happiness.

Françoise Sagan

feeling competitive? Am I? I figure it's best to keep it mellow. If the other car is in front of me, I don't try to pass. But I do try, pretty hard, to keep up. If I'm in front, it's a little trickier. I don't actually want to be passed, but it depends on what's behind me. I won't tolerate being passed by a pickup truck. I know that they can be fast and powerful and their drivers may be aggressive, but in these circumstances being passed by a truck goes against my belief system. I have a responsibility to pull away until they disappear from my rear view mirror and then keep on pulling till they don't come back into it. This is a character flaw, of course, and makes me go faster than I really want to and accept more danger than I'd like, but there it is. If the car behind me is a hot hatch, on the other hand, or an even faster car like a Corvette, then I'm content to just try and stay ahead--mostly because if I seriously tried to pull away I'd probably kill myself, which also goes against my belief system. The truth is that etiquette in this situation demands either going slow enough to allow yourself to be passed or else fast enough so that the other driver stays entertained trying to keep up. The middle ground, the speed at which you're slower than the other driver would prefer, but too fast to allow safe passing, that's rude.

    Country roads are nice, but that kind of driving is rare for most of us. We spend most of our time behind the wheel driving on roads that are slow, crowded and regulated. People tend to drive a little faster than the posted limit, but otherwise drivers around here are quite careful. They like to obey the rules because life is simpler that way. From this perspective traffic lights are very good. Red means stop; green means go; yellow is a little annoying because you have to make a decision and that provides an opening for randomness and uncertainty to enter into it. It turns out that different drivers react differently to yellow lights! Why can't everyone be the same? Well, pretty soon cars will drive themselves and the whole problem of decision-making will disappear. Another thing that will be lost, though, is driver courtesy. Drivers around here seem to like being courteous. They love four-way stops and crosswalks, or any situation that gives them a chance to be polite. Drivers carefully stop and wait, which means, in the body language of cars, "You go ahead." "No," says the other car, "I'll wait, you go ahead." It's all very civilized.

What many drivers don't like are situations that involve uncertainty. It's hard to get rid of uncertainty, though. Even at a four-way stop, what happens if two cars arrive at the same time. Was it exactly at the same time, or was one really first? What is the polite thing to do? It's not quite clear. Even a simple right turn can involve uncertainly and calculation. Let's say the little road you're on intersects with a busier road onto which you want to turn right. Chances are you have a stop sign and the traffic on the big road does not. This is uncertain and complicated on many levels. Suppose you look left and you see another car coming your way. How far away is it? How fast is it going? Is the driver signaling to turn right? If so, can you believe that the car is actually going to turn right? Should you pull out and go--avoiding all eye contact of course--or should you wait? But if you wait, there might be more cars coming behind; if so, how long might it be before you get another chance? This is very annoying, and that's just for turning right. Heaven forefend you might want to turn left. Damn this uncertainty! Damn this necessity to think about what I am doing! I'd much rather be concentrating on something else. Why don't they put in a light here? Won't somebody just tell me what to do?

The veneer of civilization does crack occasionally, exposing more atavistic impulses. Some commuters are nervous. In the morning, they're psyched up for work, at least psyched up enough to be able to function, but they're conflicted about having to go there to that place and do that work thing at all. Consequently, they haven't left home exactly on time and now they have to worry about being late. They're liable to cut in front of you or at very least whiz past on the right. They might run red lights, just a little, so it's best if you don't rush out into the intersection immediately just as your light turns green, but of course you do that anyway, cuz you're late too. Nine hours later, after work, people are frazzled and eager to get home. Some of them are frustrated at having to be nicer at work than they really are, especially in regard to certain individuals who are just world class jerks but you have to be nice to them anyway. Under these conditions, things on the road can get competitive and courtesy may break down a little. Still, things are pretty quiet here in my town and road rage is rare.

I lived in Yemen for a while and road rage was pretty rare there too. Which is good because there are a lot of guns there and anybody can pick up a fully functional 50 caliber machine gun with no trouble provided they can come up with the cash. Traffic was pretty different in Sana'a. People tended to obey traffic lights to a degree because traffic police would hang out near them and write down your license number if they saw you running through a red light. They couldn't chase you down because they didn't have cars, but they would turn their report into the traffic court. The court couldn't send you a summons because there was no actual postal system and they couldn't call you because they didn't know your number. So they just filed the report and red-flagged your registration. Then when you came to the DMV to do anything at all, bingo. It was time to pay your fine, which by that point had become astronomical due to late payment penalties and it took hours and hours of negotiation to get it down to something you could reasonably pay. So anyway, people did obey the lights pretty much.

Everything else was random. There weren't too many stop signs and the ones that existed were pretty much ignored. Basically everyone just went where they wanted to go and it all worked out. My friend David, an old hand, said that it was like two herds of goats that happened to cross each other's path. Goats being illiterate, there were no written rules, but it worked out anyway. Traffic in Yemen was different from here, but you can't really say it was worse. Unlike in some Middle Eastern countries, women were allowed to drive in Yemen. They wore veils, though, and that was a little disconcerting. Are you sure you can see out of that? But of course they could, at least well enough. As I said earlier, driving is natural to humans, and humans everywhere are good at working out ways to avoid hitting each other. The only tricky time, the time when I didn't like to be on the road, was the late afternoon rush hour, between 5:30 and 6:30 if I remember correctly. Now you might be thinking the rush was due to people getting off work and driving home. But no. Actually the culprit was qat, a sort of mild stimulant drug that people are fond of there. Back then, Yemenis liked to get their work done in the morning. Then at about 1:00 they would adjourn to hot lunch, usually the main meal of the day. At 2:30 or so they'd get together with friends and chew qat leaves. The effects of qat are generally pleasant, you feel energized but a little spacy at the same time, sort of like washing down a lot of aspirin with several cups of coffee. Qat parties are very convivial. They begin with lots of animated discussion and free-flowing ideas about how to solve the world's problems. So the first hour or two of the party is very noisy. But then it gets quieter, people get lost in their own thoughts, and drift away into a mellow, meditative state. Houses have sitting rooms that are designed for chewing and they usually have lots of big windows. You can just sit there and look out the window and be content. People begin to leave the party, sometimes just to go outside somewhere and watch the world go by for a little while. Then as the qat effect continues to wear off, people get restless and grouchy. They're still a little speedy, but they're also getting kind of pissed off. So they all get in their cars and drive home in a hurry. It's the time of day when the streets are most crowded and the drivers are most prickly and hurried. It's a very interesting time to be on the road--lots of jerky starts and stops and lots of horns going off.

    I've said that drivers are generally very courteous in the town where I live now. There's one particular place, however, where courtesy has been known to fail. It's at an intersection in a residential neighborhood. The two streets that intersect are of that in-between variety, not really busy, but not really quiet either. The speed limit is the standard residential 25 mph, but both the streets are fairly wide and most of the drivers on them are just passing through the neighborhood to get to somewhere else. So most cars are actually traveling in the thirties. It's the kind of place where traditionally we have had four-way stops. But a few years ago, the city made a traffic circle by building a small round island in the middle of the intersection and placing a Yield sign on all four incoming lanes. Angry letters to the editor began to appear almost immediately. People hated it. They claimed it was monstrously unsafe and complained about being forced to go blocks out of their way to avoid this obvious deathtrap. Stories abounded of cars that failed to slow down for the intersection or that seemed to actually speed up as they approached. It seemed that drivers who were perfectly docile about stopping at stop signs were enraged by the requirement that they might have to yield to a car already in the circle. Their solution was simply to step on the gas and make sure they got to the intersection first. I witnessed this myself once or twice. This shows how thin the veneer can be and how quickly uncertainty can turn to competition and thence to aggression. "If the system won't tell me exactly what to do," these drivers seem to saying, "if anyone tries to make me think and make decisions, then I'll just go insane and ram into someone--and it won't be my fault."

Recently, the city has decided to remove this circle, which was, in fact, quite small and weird. But they are also planning to build another traffic circle on the edge of town at the intersection of two faster roads. The area is still half rural. Opposition is fierce. Roundabouts are deadly, a wasteful and foolish idea. Why can't we just have a light there? Given the undeniable fact that there are tens or hundreds of thousands of successful and safely functioning roundabouts in the world, this view is interesting. It suggests that drivers here in my town are different, that they won't be able to manage roundabouts, that they will make bad decisions with disastrous results. This can't really be true, can it? It's true that many drivers here are unfamiliar with roundabouts. They may be afraid of them and fear could conceivably cause bad decision-making. But wouldn't drivers just be extra cautious the first few times? As they became familiar with the new intersection, wouldn't their comfort and confidence levels rise? You'd think so, but I guess you can't be sure. If a person is really determined to never have to think, maybe they'll always prefer a light to a roundabout.

I learned to drive on roundabouts in Europe, including a giant one in the middle of Paris followed two days later by one next to a car rental office in England, where the traffic in circle was much faster-moving and where the cars were all circling in the opposite direction. Yo! I haven't forgotten either one of those. Those first experiences were scary. I've since driven through hundreds of roundabouts, mostly in other countries, and for me they work awfully well. If traffic is light, you zip on through without stopping. If traffic is heavy, you wait your turn. And even when traffic is super heavy, they still work well enough, especially the modern ones that combine an underpass for the heaviest through traffic with a roundabout above.

Roundabouts are often smooth but they are not necessarily easy. In most places around the world where I've driven, you have to think about what you're doing if you're going to survive on the road. I'm thinking of Spain, Italy and France a few years back and more recently Cyprus and Turkey. Driving is a kind of dance and the dance moves are different everywhere you go. You have to learn them. Then you have to pay attention and apply what you've learned. And generally, human dances aren't slow. Folk dancing isn't slow, the jitterbug wasn't slow, and neither was doin' the locomotion, to say nothing of the moves on today's Dancing with the Stars. The driver's dance is usually fast too. It's a physical and mental workout and you need to be up for it or else you should stay home.

But I'm afraid that in my part of the world, and in the U.S. in general, people don't want to think about their driving and they believe that to have any fun driving is fundamentally evil. Sort of like a giant, nationwide, no dancing cult. They want cars to act like other machines, like dishwashers for example. You turn them on and they do the work while you occupy yourself with something else entirely. You don't even have to remember to turn the machine off because when the work is done the machines turn themselves off. I have to say I hate that. It's boring.

On I-5 in Oregon between Salem and Portland, there are

three lanes in each direction. The middle lane is the most popular, but often enough, every lane is full. And everyone is going the same speed. Everyone has their cruise control set for 69 to 73 mph. What's that about? Well, it's because the limit is 65 and everyone wants to go as fast as possible while still obeying the rules. It's not that they want to break the speed law, not at all, it's that we all know that the real limit is the enforcement threshold, which is almost always 5-9 mph higher than the posted limit. (In fact, the threshold may be even higher than that. I personally like to think that patrol officers are looking for specifically for reckless behavior, rather than at speed per se. But of course I am a known goofball.) But with everyone going at about the same speed the whole experience is just massively boring. Aggressive freeway drivers, of which I am definitely not one, are forced to do much weaving around if they want to go even moderately faster than 73. These drivers spend a lot of time in the right lane, actually, which is supposed to be the slowest but which tends to be the fastest, at least for short stretches, because nobody wants to drive there because that's supposedly the slow lane and they want to drive fast.

And the final thing is that on a modern freeway, considering the width of the lanes, the limited access and the radii of the curves, 73 mph is not fast, not fast at all, it's slow. So in reality, everyone is going too slow and they're doing it in every lane. The whole thing drives me insane. I don't fight it, though, cuz there's no point. I just do what everyone else does.

What this all comes down to is that for many drivers, there are two propositions that govern every trip by car. The first is that what matters most is the destination since that's the reason they're in the car at all. The second is that they'd rather not be in the car at all, but since they have to be there for a while the driving experience should require as little of their attention as possible, which will leave them free to concentrate on other things that are more pleasant. If you ask a cross section of people what they think about self-driving cars, you will find that a large percentage of them think it's a fantastic idea. Yes, they will be afraid that it won't really work; they don't quite trust Google; they are leery of ceding control to a

The last days of an unloved traffic circle. The island remains, but its days are numbered. The four Yield signs have already been replaced by four Stop signs. The new instruction is clearer.

Finally, we can all get back to just stopping. Which is great for people who like to stop...and who don't like to think.

system they don't fully understand. But the basic idea? Many people love it. I like it too. Only my dream is of a system where only certain roads would have full automation--meaning that once you're on that road, you sit back and the system drives you to where you want to go. The automated road system might correspond roughly to the current network of interstate highways plus a few other major routes. But then the rest of the roads would be normal. The way this dream goes, the automatic system would be so popular that the rest of the roads would have hardly any traffic and a person in a Jaguar could go wild. (My other dream, of course, is that trucks would disappear because all freight moved by train, that the number of cars on the road was magically reduced to about ten percent of what it is presently, and that the posted speed limit on the interstate was 150. That would be fine. But I digress.)

In the real world, what strikes me is that that we have too much focus on destinations and we don't pay enough attention to the joy of driving. Now I know that some people say that they just don't enjoy driving, period. I can understand having that attitude toward certain kinds of driving, of course. But as far as the basic experience of making a car go, of invoking the magic that lets you fly faster than the wind, I don't actually understand how anyone could not like that.

Sometimes I think that the basic problem with driving is the same as the basic problem with life: too much focus on destinations and goals. Get rid of them, I say, root them out! Obliterate those suckers! I know it sounds radical, maybe even impossible, and do you know why it sounds radical and impossible? Because it is radical and impossible; goals and destinations are hard-wired into us. We can no more get rid of them than we can get rid of our vertebrae. The only thing that we can do is to simultaneously keep in mind that they are illusions. None of us are really going anywhere in any ultimate sense; we're always headed back to where we started from; we're all just looping.

Now some people may not want to hear that. Some will say it's obviously not true; others will say it's too depressing to contemplate. I'll deal with the first problem first. How can I say it's all loops? Doesn't everybody know that there are actually three basic kinds of trips--by car or any other means--and that loops are only one of them? A loop is when you go from point A to point B to point C to points D, E, F, etc. in a more or less circular fashion, which eventually brings you back to point A. Fine. But life is not all loops, some would say. There are also trips there-and-back, lots of them. That's when you go from point A to point B and then back to point A. And finally, there are one-way trips, where you go from point A to point B and then you just stay there.

The problem with trying to divide our drives into these three types is that in terms of our actual experience in the world, they're all the same. Most obviously, the so-called there-and-back trips are just a special kind of loop that happens to involve a more limited set of named routes and vectors. Here's how it works. The trip out leads from point A to point B to point C to point D to some point of farthest distance that we might call point E. Then we turn around, and as we do so, we create a little loop. We then start back toward point A. However, when we reach the place on the map that we called point D, we find that it's not really the same as it was when we passed it before. For one thing we are a slightly different person and we are in a slightly or hugely different mood than when we passed there earlier. For another thing the view we have of the scene is totally different. The same objects are there, but we tend to take notice of an entirely different subset of objects and even when we see the same objects we see the opposite sides of them. And the challenges to the driver are also different. To call this the same "place" as point D is fine if you are operating entirely in the abstract realm; but if you're a living, breathing entity, it's insane. You experience a little bit of point D, but there's also a bunch of new stuff, enough so that we have to give it a new name: point F. Then comes Point C/G, then comes Point B/H, then you're back to A. It's a loop.

But what about one-way trips, where you start at point A and go to point B and just stay there? That can't possibly be a loop. Well in a certain sense that's absolutely true. Of course it's not a loop, not stated that way in those terms. But that's not the only way to look at it. Let's think about actually making a one-way trip in real life. Let's say you get fed up with life in Birmingham and you decide to move to Eau Claire. First you figure out what stuff to take with you and whether you have to carry it all yourself or pay someone else to carry it. Then you get in your car and drive north till you get there. Abstractly, your trip ends when you cross the Eau Claire city limits, but really it doesn't end till you move into your new home or apartment. So there you are; you started at point A and now you're at point B. But as soon as you move in you realize you need some stuff, some food, some cleaning supplies and a curtain rod. So you go out and make some kind of loop from your apartment to Walmart and back. You have a new job in Eau Claire and maybe a new boyfriend or girlfriend. You start making a lot more trips--loops, that is--related to those two. And at a certain point you realize that even though Eau Claire is different from Birmingham in some ways, it's awfully similar in others. And even though your job is better, it's still just a job and it's kind of annoying at times. You've now got some things that you didn't have before, but now you want other things. And even though your new relationship is better than your old one, you're still you and you still have some of the same tendencies to screw things up as you did before back in your last relationship. You now have a new place to call home, a new center from which you venture out for one reason or another and then return to rest. But that's what you had before. You went from Point A to Point B, but now that Point B has become your new point A. You've traveled all right, all the way from one place to another, and the trip was interesting and eventful, but the essence of the trip was to travel from point A to point A. You have made, I submit, a loop. And that's not something to be depressed about because loops are fine. In fact, loops are wonderful. There are joys and pleasures all along the way, new challenges, new opportunities to love and be loved, new chances to do meaningful and rewarding work.

    Point A is not a place on the map. Actually, point A is you. It's part of a loop, but it isn't located at any one particular place in the loop; it's at every point. It's everywhere you are and it keeps changing moment by moment. So pay attention to what you're doing when you're driving (or bicycling or riding the train.) Forget destinations, because you'll never get there, and you've already been there anyway.

Chapter 9: Driving Properly

Why properly? Well, the Jaguar is a British car, English in fact, and it was from England that we Americans first learned our manners, such manners as we have. So we'll need to address this. Driving properly is not the same as driving well. Almost everyone in the U.S. drives well; just ask us and we'll tell you. At least seventy per cent of us think we are above average. But driving well in the United States is a curious admixture of stuff that mostly consists of not causing or getting into accidents. Driving properly is more interesting.

Proper is a quintessential British word. It has two related meanings. First, it can be used to describe behavior or situations that are in accord with conventionally expected standards. Used in this sense, it means that you follow the rules. I personally love to follow rules. Rules minimize personal decision making and when things do inevitably go wrong, there's no way I'm going to get the blame. Very relaxing. In terms of driving, for example, if you follow the rules, you don't ever have to worry about getting a huge fine. You might still be killed on the road, but it won't be your fault. Americans love to think of ourselves as rebels and outlaws because this is exciting and romantic, but of course most of us are more comfortable just following the rules. The only problem with rules is that some of the most important ones are unwritten. It takes a lifetime of struggle to figure that one out.

In some ways, the concept of propriety is easier in Britain because convention is much stronger and clearer there. (In case you don't know, the basic rule of propriety in Britain is never to say anything real about anything, not ever, but especially not at tea time.) The paradox, though, is that even though everyone knows pretty clearly what proper behavior is, beneath the surface there's an awful lot of other stuff going on. Propriety is a middle class sort of a deal and the middle class can seem like a very orderly and well-walled space. But actually the walls are riddled with little half-hidden doorways, making it possible to slip out for an afternoon or a weekend and either mess about in the lower classes or pretend to belong to the upper classes. Both of those are places where propriety has much less sway.

But I must resist the temptation to discuss proper behavior in general. The topic is too grand. We are talking here about the proper way to drive a Jaguar. First we will talk about this in the sense of proper than I have already mentioned, the matter of conforming to society's rules and expectations. But we also have to talk about the proper driving of Jaguars in another sense of the word, the sense in which it refers to some mixture of words like genuine, suitable, true, and appropriate. This sense derives from the same root as the word property and it contains a hint of the concept of ownership, a suggestion that it describes that which is genuine and true because it pertains to your own true self. As I say, we'll get to that later. First, we must deal with society's expectations.

The first thing to understand is that cars can create expectations in others just on the basis of their category or shape. These expectations don't always bear fruit, but yet, in general, when we see a minivan ahead we do groan a little. We expect a slow driver and we are correct in that assumption more often than not. Society also expects Prius drivers to go slow. This is not unreasonable; we assume that the driver values economy--that's why they have a Prius--and we know that quick acceleration and high speed drive fuel economy down. We may also expect that the driver is unlikely to go fast around corners because the driver probably does not value handling and may not enjoy corners much anyway. And a Prius is not going to win any drag races. It's 0-60 time of around ten seconds is one or two seconds slower than the great majority even of small cars. So if other drivers expect them to be slow, that expectation is not totally irrational. But of course they are capable of going fast; their top speed is around 100 mph and it's perfectly possible that a Prius driver might pass another car once in a while. According to Prius owners, however, other drivers sometimes react badly to this. Hybrids are supposed to be slow; hence if a driver is passed by one, humiliation occurs. The passed driver may then stomp on the gas of their 'real' car and try to erase this humiliation by getting back ahead of the Prius, even if it means engaging in some irregular behavior. Someday, when cars drive themselves, human expectations won't matter; the cars will have to negotiate these things among themselves.

The other side of the coin is that some cars are expected to go fast. Speed modified small cars are one example. A regular Honda Civic creates no special expectation at all; it's too common, too mainstream, we don't really expect much of anything. But people like to modify Civics to make them go faster and generally they also want other people to know that they have done this. Modified Civics have special go fast parts that stick out here and here, they have decals on darkly tinted windows, and always have overlarge rear exhausts. The drivers of these cars, if they are to be in sync with the expectations they create, need to drive fast, pass on the right, make a lot of noise, engage in informal drag races, and generally do what rodders have always done. This is the proper style for the car. When the driver is being slow and careful for some reason, the car is not being properly operated.

The Nissan 350Z is another example of a car that is expected to go fast--at least by some people. I noticed when I drove mine on two lane highways that sometimes other cars would actually slow down when I came up behind them. And I'm not talking about zooming in so as to appear almost instantly on the other driver's rear bumper, because in fact I rarely ever do that. Even when I was not going all that fast, relative to the car ahead, the driver saw the shape of my car and just assumed that I wanted to pass, that I would and should pass, and that the responsibility of other drivers was to make that as easy as possible for everyone. I found it a little disconcerting. This happened on a few occasions when I in fact didn't particularly want to pass. Then on other occasions (just two actually) I also noticed a kind of opposite behavior. I'd be at a stoplight and when the light turned green the SUV or sedan next to me would give a great roar and blast off, gleefully hoping to show me what for. This never happened to me in my Miata or any more normal car that I might have been driving. The question was what to do in these situations, situations which are caused mostly just by the appearance of my car and not by anything I may have done. In the situation where expectations caused the other driver to invite me to pass, the only proper thing to do was accept. It was generally what I wanted to do anyway and even if passing the car hadn't been my immediate intention, how could I in good grace refuse? In the case of the stoplight racers, things were more complicated.

As I mentioned, both times it happened the other car was pretty ordinary: one was a fairly old Taurus and the other was some midsize SUV with a big motor but also lots of weight. They just weren't fast cars; the Taurus wasn't an SHO, as far as I could tell, and the SUV was some GM or Chrysler product, certainly no Cayenne and not even a Lexus or Mercedes. So there I was. What was the proper course--compete or ignore? My response to both of these situations was to compete. Even though I had not intended to race, it seemed to me that I had a responsibility. If I was going to drive a 350Z, I was going to have to act like a 350Z driver; otherwise I should be driving a Saturn. Now I have mentioned the word responsibility and maybe some readers are also thinking of that word. Maybe they are thinking that stoplight competitions are inherently irresponsible and dangerous and that the proper course was to ignore the challenge. There is something to this line of reasoning, of course, but I should mention that in both of these

Driving Properly

cases part of my decision to compete involved an awareness that winning would be easy and fairly quick, as indeed it turned out to be. Had the other car been a more powerful one, a hot Mustang for example, I like to think I would have let it go, maybe hoping for a rematch sometime in a safer venue.

In his book *A New Earth: Awakening to Your Life's Purpose*, Eckhart Tolle suggests three states of being that we should strive for: acceptance, enjoyment and enthusiasm. Actually, he calls them 'modalities of awakened being.' I wasn't sure what that meant. So I went to my online dictionary and looked that up. I found out that according to Babylon, 'modalities of awakened being' are 'budzone są formy.' But Google Translate disagrees; it says that they are 'modalności przebudzeniu.' So to end my confusion I went to WorldLingo.com. I knew they would be accurate because there was a character named Rhonda Lingo in a novel I wrote when I was younger. Since they agree with Babylon, I'm sticking with budzone są formy. And how, some of my more perceptive readers will be asking, does it help to machine translate this phrase into Polish, even if we spoke Polish, which most of us don't? Well, the answer to that is simple, I don't speak Polish either. And remember, Eckhart Tolle was born in Germany and Germany is close to Poland, maybe a little too close. So let's continue.

It turns out that if you had to choose three words to help you drive your Jaguar properly, you could do a lot worse than acceptance, enthusiasm and enjoyment. Enjoyment is the key, of course. There's no reason to buy or drive a Jaguar unless you're going to enjoy it. You might enjoy hurtling along at illegal speeds, you might enjoy just sitting in it in your driveway listening to the stereo. You might enjoy arriving at the house where the party is and comparing your car to all the others. You might enjoy driving sedately down a country lane lined with cherry blossoms. Personally I enjoy taking my front license plate off and putting it back on. By buying a Jaguar you have made a statement about how you feel about driving, that driving is something that can be savored. You've chosen the Jaguar because Jaguars are made with that in mind. You know that the aim of some cars is simply to transport someone from point A to point B as unobtrusively as possible--as if the trip never really existed--but you want more than that, so you don't want those cars. You want the ride to be a pleasure. So, rule number one for proper driving: Don't forget to enjoy it

Acceptance is also a good concept to keep in mind. The list of things you have to accept in Jaguarland is endless. You already know most of them: the initial cost and the depreciation, the repair costs, the pity and incomprehension in the eyes of some of your friends, your feelings of insecurity when you see a BMW M5 or a Panamera, and the list goes on. One more thing you'll have to accept is that the world sometimes seems to be conspiring to make driving less and less of a pleasure no matter what car you drive. Acceptance here means recognizing that this tendency exists and giving a certain amount of time and effort to actively working against or around it. Make the effort to find the good places to drive. They're getting rarer, but they're out there and they're worth seeking for. Also on the list is acceptance of the speed expectations of other drivers. You may get the occasional invitation to drive fast. You may have to pass someone; you may have to drag race once in a great while. You are going to have to accept some of these invitations, keeping in mind that they are not challenges whose only possible outcomes are victory or death. You are required to accept them, but you are not required to take them too seriously, that would not be the Jaguar way. Take them seriously enough to show respect, but keep in mind that you have an obligation as a Jaguar owner to be just a bit less serious than drivers of some other cars, especially Corvettes, Porsches, and Ferraris--serious cars for serious people. If you were that kind of person, you'd have one of those cars. So if a Corvette comes up behind you and seems to want to pass, yes, you do need to step on the gas; but only because it will be more fun that way for both of you. Make other drivers work; they'll appreciate it. Just don't take it too seriously.

I must recognize here that there is another way of responding to other drivers who may want to race you in one manner or another. According to this school of thought, which I will call the patrician's view, the correct response of a Jaguar owner is to maintain aplomb at all times and never be rushed. In other words, when some yahoo in a semi-fast jalopy guns it up and rushes ahead of you, the proper thing is simply to continue at one's own pace and let the other car go, secure in the knowledge that if you did wish to compete in such a foolish contest, which of course you don't, you could just put your foot down and blow the other car away. Well, I can't really argue with this view; conceptually it's beautiful. I'll be glad to tip my hat to anyone who can bring it off. I can't quite do it myself though, because I don't have that much confidence, which suggests that I don't have the makings of a good patrician.

And putting aside my personal issues, I also have two philosophical objections, one aesthetic and one epistemological. First, confidence like that borders on smugness and even though smugness is very British I don't see it as very Jaguarish. It's too ugly. In fact this is one of the reasons that Jaguar was successful in the first place. Large swaths of British culture was/is just plain ugly; William Lyons made his fortune by offering the British public something finer and more elegant. Second, the attitude borders on solipsism. It's something like, I know I could win because I know it, and therefore it must be true. The fact is that you are not really alone in the world. Unless you at some point mash your foot to the floor, you don't really know what the results of that would be. Of course these are just practical and logical objections and the patrician view is largely a matter of style. We know that style can trump logic. It happens all the time. Which is fine with me, so if you can bring it, bring it.

But enough about acceptance, let's go back to begeisterung. Begeisterung is German for the Turkish coşku, which in Polish is entuzjazm, which as you will remember is another one of the three Budzone są formy. I don't know why Eckhart Tolle believes in entuzjazm because my wife hasn't explained it to me yet. But in Jaguarland, you may find that enjoyment and acceptance by themselves don't quite add up. You're going to need to bring some coşku to the party, some personal energy, some oomph. The reason you need to keep your Jaguar moving right along is that you need to keep yourself moving right along. If you don't make a grab for the enjoyment, it might not be there. Buying a black cowboy hat with silver doodads is one thing; you also have to make the effort to wear it. And without entuzjazm, your acceptance might devolve into whining and regret. You know that patrician view I was just talking about, the one that makes no sense? That fact is that if you enjoy it and accept its limitations and you have entuzjazm, it's almost sure to work for you.

And this brings us back to the proper meaning of proper, not the one that suggests that you follow convention, but the one that suggests that you drive according to your own true self. There is a way of driving that you own, that is your property. You have to drive that way for the sake of enjoyment; you have to drive that way for the sake of enthusiasm. In a Jaguar, you will likely find that it includes both pace and grace, to quote two Jaguar marketing terms from the Lyons era. It includes, also, the notion of driving according to your own true mood at the moment; you are not required to be consistent in your enthusiasms or your enjoyment. If you feel like driving slowly, your cat will be very content to assist you in this. If you feel like driving fast, it will also oblige.

If you are feeling suicidal, though, you don't really need a Jag. Any old car will do. And speaking of anguish and despair, what about romantic relationships? Can a Jaguar help with that? That question deserves a chapter of its own.

Chapter 10: Relationships: The Jaguar Effect

How often have you heard someone say "I never had any luck with romance till I got my Jag?" Or maybe, "Man, since I bought the Jag I've been beating them off with a stick!" Or how about, "Only when I got my Jaguar did I find true love." I don't know about you, but I've never heard anybody say anything like that. And why haven't I? It would be great to hear something like that. I'd love it. It could be that I've led a sheltered life or that the people I know are too discreet to speak of such things. Or it may be because no one in real life actually says (or even thinks) things like that about Jaguars or any other cars. But if that's true, what are we to make of quotations like the following?

Jacob Joseph, writing for *CarBuzz*:
> *The XK owner is not concerned with 'swag', as he knows that a real lady prefers sophistication. He likes nice and stylish things but is not so insecure that he needs to show off. It's not difficult to see why this kind of image would make the owner of such a car appealing to women.*
> (http://www.carbuzz.com/news/2012/)

Petrina Gentile, writing for *MSN Autos*:
> *And when it comes to attracting the opposite sex, no other vehicle comes close to the Jaguar XKR*

Coupe...Everywhere I drove...guys followed me, stopping to chit chat about the XKR. They even rolled down windows at stoplights to find out what I was driving...This Jaguar is a bait to trap men, young and old.

(http://autos.ca.msn.com/)

Henry Manney III, writing for *Road and Track* back in the day and referring to the Jaguar E-Type:
The greatest crumpet-catcher known to man.

Are these writers revealing the truth of things, exposing what we all suspected but that most Jaguar owners have chosen not to reveal--at least to me? Or are they just blowing hot air? I think we have to be skeptical. These three characters may write about Jaguars and have certainly test driven Jaguars, but it's not clear whether they have ever actually owned one. And how can you trust writers anyway? A writer can say almost anything--I should know. More to the point, when professional automotive writers write about cars they have to wear their automotive writer hats. Writers are compelled to tell stories; they need to entertain and get their readers' attention. It helps in this to tell people what they want to hear, to feed their dreams. And what a dream it is: buy this car and find love. Yes! No matter how you feel right now, happiness is within your grasp. And it is so simple; just get together some money and buy the right car. Things will fall into place. And if you don't have quite enough money, credit is available.

We know that dreams and reality don't always coincide. I mean, maybe yours do, but I think most people's don't. So yeah, we know it's not nearly so simple as what I have described, not quite as simple as our three writers might make it seem. But I still think they are onto something, all three of them. I don't know Petrina Gentile at all, but I don't think she's lying. I think that when she drove around in an XKR, she got a little more attention than she normally did. Remember in an earlier chapter when I recounted a couple of experiences my wife and I have had in our Jaguar? People do come up to you and talk. And remember the blonde mystery girl in *American Graffiti*?

The one in the light blue '56 Thunderbird? She got attention. The audience never gets to know her, never even gets to see her standing or walking. All we know is that she has Suzanne Somers' face and drives the T-bird. Either one might have been enough, but the combination was killer. Petrina Gentile doesn't live in a movie, but there is a ring of truth in her story, just as there is a clear sort of mythic truth about the blue car girl in the film.

Henry Manney III, who many have called the best automtive writer of his time, is doing a bit of a schtick in his quote, playing the part of an irreverent observer, an American who has traveled a bit. Back in his time, Europe still symbolized a higher level of sophistication and worldliness than America. Manney shows his sophistication by addressing the subject of cars and sex directly and also by letting us know that he's traveled and that he's learned a little British slang. I will leave for individual readers the task of judging on their own what level of offensiveness the word 'crumpet' carries here, but linguistically and stylistically speaking, I know a well-turned phrase when I see one. But is it true? Or more specifically, does Manney think it is true? Or is he hiding behind his observer status and not really saying what he thinks, just commenting on those funny Brits and what they seem to think? I don't know. And it's possible Manney didn't know either. Has he personally experienced or personally witnessed a seduction that was consummated through the good offices of an E-Type? It doesn't really matter. What he has done is given expression, in a charming and memorable way, to an idea that resonates with a large number of people, whether they actually believe it or not.

Jacob Joseph takes a different, less direct, approach. Although he is addressing the same general topic that Manney did, he has changed the terms of the central question. Neither writer states the question explicitly in these short excerpts, but we are not fools, we readers, we know what the two questions are. To assert that the Jaguar E-Type is 'the greatest crumpet catcher known to man' is an answer the question "How can I get a hot chick to have sex with me?" But when Joseph says "it's not difficult to see why this kind of image would make the owner of such a car appealing to women" that's the answer to a very different question, something like: "What effect will my having a Jaguar have on potential partners?" It's tempting to see the difference in terms of twenty-first century post-feminist discourse. Joseph is going to stay far away from the objectification of women; hence, no crumpet talk. And no way is he going to suggest that women are so silly and foolish as to be attracted merely by pretty things. No, women in this context are rational and perceptive, quite capable of knowing what they want. They will be attracted to Jaguar drivers because they will recognize someone of taste, discernment and emotional maturity, someone they could be serious about, at least to the extent of...having sex.

The Joseph approach may be more appropriate for contemporary times. It is a bit bloodless, though, and a bit idealized. My own view is that women do sometimes act silly, sometimes do make foolish decisions, and are sometimes affected by their hormones, and also that it is not at all sexist to think so. It is only sexist to pretend that men are not equally silly, foolish and hormonal. I have even entertained the remote possibility that men are actually sillier and more foolish, at least in general, than women are. But still, one can understand perfectly why Joseph is being careful to avoid the stereotype that sees women as brainless simpletons, mindlessly attracted to pretty things. (And thank god men aren't like that either! Oh, but wait. Men are like that. They're exactly like that. But I digress.) In any case Joseph's more reasoned approach is also more appropriate to today's Jaguars, which are fine and beautiful things but which have considerably more subtlety than the E-Type.

What it comes down to is that image and identity matter. We are who we are and we want what we want, both in cars and in partners. Whether a car will help us get what we want is hard to say. As we saw in Chapter 3, a person's choice of vehicle does say something about that person and there's no way we can avoid this. If you drive a Leaf, a person who admires green transportation is going to have a little extra

Relationships: The Jaguar Effect

interest in you. We could say similar things about pickup trucks, SUV's, Camrys or whatever. Even if you drive something you didn't personally choose, like an old sedan handed down from a relative, that in itself says something about you, to say nothing of what it might say about the clan from which you have sprung.

Now of course as I write this chapter, I've been thinking about my own history of relationships and cars. I had a hand-me-down Plymouth Valiant once, but I never really tried it out as an attractant to possible romantic partners; I was too busy dealing with graduate school and with the partner I already had. She was a handful. A few years before though, around the time I met her, I'd had a Triumph TR3, so now I'm trying to think: "Did the car have anything to do with us getting together?" Naw. I think I know what it was and it wasn't the car. So we'll need to make an "It-wasn't-the-car" column on my scorecard and put one checkmark in it to start.

Eventually my Valiant years ended and so did that relationship. When my next serious relationship started, I had no car and was getting around by bicycle. That'll be checkmark number two in the negative column.

The relationship after that, however, was a little different. I had a TR4 by then, and I think that particular woman kinda liked it. She didn't mind being seen in it and she once told me she enjoyed the view when the hood was up and I was bent over the engine bay--probably trying in vain to adjust the worn out SU carburetors. So I think we can make a new column. Let's call it "Might have had something to do with it" and put one checkmark there.

In my current relationship, which has lasted quite a while now, my partner has seen a Miata, a 350Z and now the Jaguar. She did seem to like going out in the Miata and after we had done that for a while, she did agree to marry me. In fact we drove away from the wedding reception in that car. So there's that. Of course I also offered her flowers, expensive perfume and an antique cut diamond. But hey, the car might have had something to do with it. This is the same woman who was approached by some guy in a supermarket parking lot one time when she was driving the XKR. He wanted to say how much he liked her car. Just being friendly I suppose.

So for all of you out there who are either single or acting that way, the chances are good that getting a Jaguar will help you get noticed--maybe not by every single potential partner in the world--but by that subset of potentials who appreciate fast, beautiful cars, which is likely to be a pretty interesting group.

Suppose, though, that a person is not single, that a person is maybe even married, maybe even married for quite some time. And suppose that this person gets the idea of buying a Jaguar. Wouldn't it be great if the other person in the relationship were to say: "A Jaguar!? That's fantastic! Let's go look at one now!" Unfortunately, that doesn't always happen. Sometimes the other person says something like: "We have a perfectly good car now. Why would we want to waste our money getting something more expensive?" And sometimes, that other person doesn't even have to speak because the person who is thinking about the Jag doesn't even dare mention it, knowing in advance how negative the response is likely to be. Either way, we are entering deep water here. The Jaguar is not playing its traditional role of attracting a partner. Instead, the Jag is a potentially disruptive force. In its crudest form the question becomes: "What's more important, the car or me?" In this form the question is not healthy, since it only has one answer, which goes something like "Well, you're both satisfying, but the car gives me a less grief and it's a lot easier to fix."

But let's back up a little. One of our main goals here is to manage this situation in such a way as to prevent that 'either-or' question from ever coming up. To do this, the person who is considering the Jaguar has to be proactive and has to pretend to be emotionally mature. This last part is especially important. The other party will almost certainly be suspicious. They'll know you're faking, but there's a good chance that they'll fall for it anyway. So that's the basic strategy. Before we go any further, let's look at the range of possible responses to one partner's revelation about wanting a Jaguar. We know what the best-case response is and we have an idea of the worst, but there is always a range of middle possibilities as well. Here's a longer list, ranked roughly from best response to worst.

1. You read my mind! I just saw a great deal on a 2011 XJL. Or are you thinking of a new one?

This one's pretty positive, yes? Especially compared to what your current partner might say? The only problem here might be that the other member of the pair was actually thinking of an XK rather than the XJ. But that's the kind of problem that gives value and meaning to life. They'll work it out.

2. A Jaguar, really? Do they still make Jaguars?

This is a noncommittal response, but it might not be too bad. The responder could be just stalling before stating a preference for a Mercedes (bad) but on the other hand the person is at least aware of old Jaguars (good) and may be curious to at least look at a new one (very good).

3. That would be crazy. We don't need a Jaguar!

A seemingly negative answer, but not necessarily so. In absolute terms, no one really needs a Jaguar, so that part of the response in fact leads directly to the question of whether we might *want* a Jaguar, which of course we do. And as far as the "crazy" part is concerned, crazy is an ambiguous word. When it is used to describe the things we have done or might do in life, it has positive as well as negative connotations. Most people have a sense that sometimes it's good to be a little crazy.

4. Yes...either that or a Maserati.

This is both good and bad. You might think it's good that the two partners are more or less on the same playing field. You might think it's good that they have similar tastes. But do they really? Maseratis are fast and exotic, but some of the older Cambiocorsas and the newer Gran Turismos are pretty ugly. They may score well on excitement but lower on elegance. They are not the same. Plus, as we saw in Chapter 1, there are a lot of low mileage high priced used Masers out there. Whatever that might mean, it's suspicious. Hopefully a few test drives would sort things out for this couple. It won't be the end of the world if they end up in a Quattroporte; but if they get in a big fight and eventually have to compromise on a Lexus, that would be sad.

5. A Jaguar? I don't know. I don't think I'd be comfortable in one of those.
Ouch. Not good. What this response really means is that the responder is worried that the couple's peer group would not be impressed and might actively disapprove. But there is still hope here. This is a fear response, almost an instinctive one. It may be the first response that comes out, but other, more reasoned responses might surface later. Through discussion and emotional maturity (assuming you can bring it off) it's always possible that fears could be assuaged.

6. Honey, that kind of car is so impractical. (Senario A)
There are two possibilities here, both of them bad. The first is that we might have a situation similar to #4 above, except that the speaker is really serious. Instead of the possibly ambiguous word 'crazy' they are bringing on the deadly concept of 'practicality'. This indicates that the responder is truly a practical person who values efficiency and sees the world in terms of clear and controllable parameters. In terms of total cost of ownership, this person is saying, Car A costs $X per 100 miles driven while Car J costs almost $2X to go the same distance. Case closed. This is daunting, of course, and hard to argue with. Practical people can be impressed by superior engineering and technology and that's a possible route, but it could easily backfire and you'd end up with just another German or Japanese car. The only hope here is that while the person is answering from their practical, bean counting part of their personality, the person may also have another side, a side that is usually censored but which could possibly be coaxed out into the open, possibly with the aid of small to moderate amounts of alcohol.

7. Honey, that kind of car is so impractical. (Senario B)
The other possibility is that the word 'impractical' is a red

herring. Actually the responder has also been thinking about a new vehicle, but something along the lines of a new BMW X5 or Porsche Cayenne and just hasn't gotten around to mentioning it yet. These of course are not remotely practical vehicles, but the person who wants one is hoping to get away with pretending that they are. In this case the person on the Jaguar side might be able to counter with the new for 2013 AWD XF and the AWD XJ. That could help if they're talking new cars, but if they're in the used market it's a no go.

8. We are not going to waste our money on a fancy car!

Another bad one, but also possibly not as bad as it seems. When faced with this response, it is tempting to attack the concept of waste as well as the concept of fancy. Jaguars are more than fancy; they are pleasurable and satisfying in a number of ways. And if you value what a car offers, then the money you spend on it is not wasted. Both these points need to be mentioned. Additionally, however, you may find that one of the keys here is actually the phrase 'our money.' Feelings about money are deep-seated and have the potential to poison our relationships if we allow them to. The best way to deal with the money issue is to expand the discussion to the couple's entire financial situation and what the couple's priorities actually are. Money is ridiculously neutral; no one ever actually argues about money. They argue about what to do with it, about priorities. So make a rank-ordered list of what your priorities are. Put the car on it somewhere. See if you can agree where it goes.

If either partner is contemplating a Jaguar, presumably there is some money available to make one happen. But you can spend money on zillions of things besides cars. So both partners need to make a list of what they think is most important and those lists have to be reconciled. That's life.

It may be helpful to note that there are really two sorts of expenditures, those common to the operation of the household and those that are personal to the individuals involved. Expenses such as groceries, mortgages, utilities, family vacations, and expenses related to offspring can be considered common. Both partners have a responsibility to fund these expenses. If their incomes are roughly equal, then their contributions to this category of expenses should be equal. If the two incomes are not equal, then the contribution of each should vary in roughly the same proportion as the incomes vary. But the goal is not to pour 100% of each person's income into the common fund because what you really want is not one giant pool of money but three pools: yours, mine and ours. When a partner objects to the cost of a car, you have to figure out what that really means in terms of common and personal expenses. It may mean that the partner wants more investment in the common fund, possibly for something specific like a better house, better quality groceries, nicer vacations, or more expensive schools. Or it may mean that the partner is just generally insecure about the common fund, perhaps because of previous experience. It also may mean that the partner is tired of investing too much of their own income in the common fund and is longing to have funding for more personal projects. In either case it all has to be dragged into the light and put on the list. You can't spend common funds on a car that the other person doesn't want you to have; that's part of what being in a relationship means. But you may be able set a level of contribution to the common fund that satisfies both of you and which leaves each partner with money left over to spend on whatever they wish.

Money is kind of boring, though, and that's another reason to get rid of it by buying a Jaguar. If your partner is reluctant for any reason, the critical step is to get them to actually go look at one. Photos and videos won't do it. Try to arrange for a longish test drive on a somewhat lightly traveled road. As part of the arrangement, convince the salesperson or seller not to go along. Take the time to learn the audio and temperature controls. Play a familiar radio station or something from your phone or music player. (Bring a cable!) Drive the car in interesting ways: test the brakes and acceleration, keeping in mind your partner's level of enjoyment of g-forces, high or low as it may be. On the way back, convince your partner to drive for a while. Mention the things that you really like about the car, including the things that you think are superior to your old car. But also mention one or two things that you don't like or something that you might miss about your old car. If you can't think of any, make some up. This makes you seem less like a three-year-old grabbing for a toy. On the other hand, don't be afraid to gush a little, as in "Ooh, these seats are nice!" or "Look at the depth of the color of this car!" or "Wow! This supercharger is awesome!"

Hard as it may be to believe sometimes, your partner does want you to be happy. And even the most practical partner is not immune to the Jaguar's allure. It's like anything else: if you really want it, break it down into small steps and keep after it.

And if that doesn't work with your particular partner, you can always see how your new Jaguar does at attracting a new one.

Chapter 11: Frequently Asked Questions

1. Is it socially acceptable to take a Jaguar to the Taco Bell drive through?

No.

2. Taco Time?

Yes.

3. Why doesn't my Jaguar have the leaping Jaguar hood ornament?

Possibly it was stolen while you were in the drive through line at Taco Bell. More likely, though, your car never came with one. Hood ornaments such as the leaping cat have become ever more rare, for two reasons. First, they make it difficult for carmakers to comply with pedestrian safety standards. Second, they make a very tempting target for thieves looking for a souvenir. Such thieves not only make off with the ornament but also seriously damage the hood in the process. Rolls Royce has addressed these problems by making their hood ornament retractable. It is spring-loaded and to prevent pedestrian injury it will instantly retract whenever there is forceful impact nearby. To deal with the theft issue it can also be retracted or extended by the driver from inside the car. Jaguar has not gone this route, which, all in all, may not be a bad thing.

4. No, you're not listening. Why doesn't my Jaguar have a leaping jaguar hood ornament?! I want one and I deserve one.

Sorry, I must have misheard your question. The fact is that they are easy to buy on the internet. Your only problems will be which size you want, how much you want to pay, and where you decide to drill the holes in the hood of your car. Those decisions are all up to you, oh deserving one.

5. What's the fastest you've ever driven in your Jaguar?

The speedometer said 145.

6. Where and when did you do that? Do you have proof, like a video or something?

In a safe and appropriate location. No. (Who are you anyway?)

7. What's the difference between a turbocharger and a supercharger?

Go away.

8. Nice car. Is it an XKE?

No. The last XKE was made in 1974. My car is a 2004.

9. Does your car have the Jaguar V-12?

No. No. No. Jaguar stopped making their V-12 in 1996. See Chapter 2. The motor in my car is an AJ V8, specifically the AJ34S. This question shows clearly that you haven't been paying the least attention. However, I must say that your obsession with the V-12 is normal and healthy. The fact that

This is an E-Type (XKE) engine from the 1961-71 era. To feed its six cylinders, it has three SU carburetors, visible here at the top of the photo. Beginning in 1967 cars destined for the U.S. were 'detuned' and fitted with just two Zenith-Stromberg carbs.

The Jaguar V-12 was used in E-types from 1971 to 1974. Through various iterations, its variants powered other Jaguar models up through 1996. The first V-12's had four Zenith-Stromberg side draft carburetors; by the end they all had fuel injection.

my car does not have the V-12 is probably just another reason you're glad you don't own it.

10. Given that your car doesn't have the Jaguar V12, does that mean that your car is basically just an expensive Ford?

Sigh. Who let you in here? The AJ V8 is a Jaguar design built with Ford money. When Ford took over Jaguar, the company was in need of an engine to replace the V-12. Ford already had a whole family of V8s and could have just started putting one or two of them into Jaguars. But, to their great credit, they did not do that. Instead they financed and supported the development of a new engine, designed and manufactured in the UK. The first AJ V8s were produced in 1996; the 2000 version made the Ward's 10 Best Engines of the World list; and the basic design is still in use today by Tata-owned JLR. From 2002 to 2006, Ford used a variant, called the AJ30/35, to power the Thunderbird and the Lincoln LS in the United States. That variant was manufactured in Lima, Ohio, but it makes more sense to say that those cars used a Jaguar engine than it does to say that Jaguars used Ford engines.

11. Have you ever drunk champagne directly from the bottle in your Jaguar?

No, but I am not going to say I never will.

12. What kind of fuel economy do you get in your Jaguar?

We don't really talk about 'economy' much...

12a. Okay, what mileage do you get?

I get around 20 mpg in mixed driving. The original EPA estimates were 16 city and 23 highway. EPA estimates hardly ever match the real world, but in this case I think they're about right. I like to imagine I could get 24 or higher if I just rolled along at 55 for a couple of hours, but I am still waiting for that

Driving at 60 mph, getting 28.8 mpg. Wow!

Driving at 75 mph and getting ridiculously low mileage. Funny how the same car can get such different mileage at different speeds. I just don't understand it.

to ever happen. In practice I've never got more than 22.8 in any kind of sustained driving. The fuel tank capacity is 19.9 gallons, so the car can go about 400 highway miles on one tank.

13. I enjoyed your presentation of oversteer and understeer in Chapter 6, but you were kind of vague about the relationships between the various forces that affect a turning vehicle. What are the relevant equations?

Vague. Right. Maybe this diagram will help. Or maybe not. How should I know? I don't actually understand any of it, except that the word Ûpoźnienie means time delay. Of course **you** probably guessed that from context, Mr or Ms Bright Eyes.

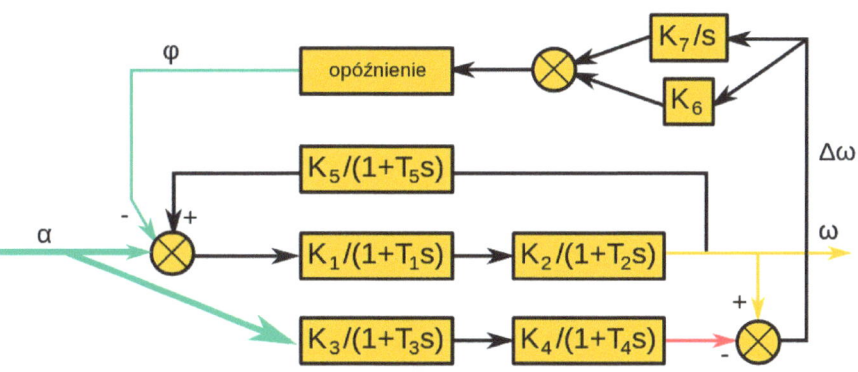

14. What are Jaguars exactly, the big cats that these cars are named after?

Jaguars are the third largest of the felines, smaller than lions and tigers but larger than leopards. They live mostly in Central and South America and are seen very occasionally in the southwestern United States. Jaguars and leopards have similar coloring and have a common genetic ancestor, but jaguars are heavier and stockier with larger spot patterns (rosettes). While most jaguars have the typical tan and black rosettes, about 6% of the population are solid black and may be referred to as

Jaguar (Panthera onca)

black panthers. Jaguars are powerful and low to the ground--sort of like an E-Type--but they are not particularly fast--sort of like an E-Type with overheating problems. The leaping jaguar hood ornament and leaping jaguar logo are not anatomically correct; they show an animal that is longer and leaner than the real thing. The jaguar face on the flat round badges that replaced the leapers is a little better, being a fair representation of what the animal might look like head on. Jaguars are ambush predators rather than chase predators and have powerful jaws, strong enough to bite through turtle shells. In fact, jaguars commonly kill by biting through the skulls of their prey.

Jaguars are good swimmers and are comfortable in the water. There's a great National Geographic video of a jaguar swimming up to a large caiman (crocodile), taking it out, and making it look easy.

15. The Jaguar XJS--the one with the V-12--was seen in a lot of big time movies and TV series, classy stuff like Columbo, Murder She Wrote, Wallander, Seinfeld, The Return of the Saint, La Femme Nikita, Weird Science, The Lovejoy Mysteries, and The Scent of a Woman. Has your car been featured in anything?

You neglected to mention that the Jaguar XJS was also featured in *Dirty Weekend, A Good Old Fashioned Orgy,* and *Diary of a Nymphomaniac*. Real classy. But, yeah, the Jaguar XKR has been in lots of things.

16. Such as?

There was one on CSI Miami once.

17. Is that it?

There was one on NCIS Los Angeles also.

18. Big whoop.

What do you mean big whoop? We're talking about the most successful TV franchise that ever happened in 2012. But if that's not enough, haven't you ever seen *Hollywood Wives: The New Generation*? And how about *Air Buddies*? or *Wo ist Fred?* or *Un ÉtÉ de canincule*? Or how about Fyodor Popov's 2004 comedy *Chetyre taksista i sobaka*?

19. Huh?

Okay, okay. *Die Another Day.* How about that?

20. Die Another Day? I happen to remember Die Another Day and I think you'll find that Pierce Brosnan had an Aston Martin Vanquish. If there was a XKR, who drove it?

Never mind. I tire of this. No more questions.

19. Ah come on, one more, tell us about all your speeding tickets.

I haven't had a ticket since the Sprite. It was a sunny day and the road was straight and empty. The Sprite needed an engine rebuild at that point; it was not fast in the least. The officer ticketed me for 65 or 68 or something. It was either revenue enhancement pressure or roadster rage. Blech.

One way to avoid tickets is to drive on roads that are so curvy that you can't go too fast. A few days ago I drove the Jag as fast as I could for a half hour or so and never got past fifty. It was hard work though.

20. Who was it who said, "Money may not buy happiness, but I'd rather cry in a Jaguar than on a bus."

That was Françoise Sagan, a French novelist who wrote her first novel, Bonjour Tristesse, while she was a teenager. It was published in 1954. She used some of her first royalties to buy a Jaguar XK120. In 1957 she crashed an Aston-Martin and was in a coma for several weeks. She didn't stop driving, though, and later owned an E-Type. There's a wonderful Helmut Newton photo of the diminutive Sagan leaning out from the behind the wheel of her Jag. It was published in French Vogue in October of 1963. Search it out.

21. And how about "I spent a lot of money on booze, birds and fast cars. The rest I just squandered."?

That would be George Best, another E-Type owner, who was born in Belfast and who earned a lot of spending money as a footballer, mainly in the sixties and seventies.

22. How can I get a Jaguar that meets my needs?

Uh...what do you mean exactly? I've got a whole chapter on buying a Jaguar. It's coming up next.

23. No, no. I don't want to buy one. I just want to get one, one that I get to ride around in as a passenger and also that I get to drive when the appropriate occasion arises. How do I arrange that?

Hm. This is getting complicated. Didn't somebody have a question about turbochargers vs. superchargers?

Chapter 12: Buying a Jaguar

Let's suppose you're interested in buying a Jaguar. Well, first of all, that's hilarious. What a sicko you are. As soon as I manage to stop laughing, maybe we can talk.

Okay. Let's get serious. If we can. Let's begin by imagining that what you're interested in is a new Jag. There are four model ranges. The XF entry level cars range from $47,000 to $99,000. The base model XF sedan gives you a 240 hp V-6, but for a mere $52,000 more you can get the XF R-S, a 550 hp rocket. (And yes, there are some steps in between.) The next car up is the XJ, a larger sedan. It ranges from $74,000 to $119,000, depending on engine and amenities. On the somewhat sportier side you can get an XK, the direct descendent of my car, for between $79,000 and $174,000. If I may be serious for a moment, these are fantastic cars. They cost a little money, but they are one of the things that money is for. Whatever your chosen model, I'd suggest that you aim for the middle of the range. You definitely need more power than the base model, but the very high end cars are perhaps a bit excessive. Of course, you might be excessive yourself, what do I know? You might want one of the new F-Types, a true 2-seater sports car offered in three model options between $69,000 and $92,000. These are October 2013 suggested retail prices for 2014 model year cars in the U.S.

Jaguar is an Indian-owned company, but it's no good going to India looking for a bargain. In Mumbai the cheapest XF is the equivalent of $74,000 and the XK cars range from $114,000 to an astronomical $305,000. If you thought that the Indian government was going to waive the import duties on Jaguars considering that the company is Indian owned, you'd be pretty wrong. How about going over to the UK where the actual factory is? Theoretically, you'd at least save the shipping. Over in Britain a base XF lists for $46,400. That's a $600 savings over the U.S. price, which probably won't finance your trip or cover your privately arranged shipping. And there is no base XK available; you have to go up to $104,000 just to get started. So forget going to England to buy your car, unless of course you want a Jaguar station wagon, called the XF SportBrake in Jag-speak. You can't get them over here at all, but across the pond there are about ten different models available, all with diesel motors. They start at $51,000 and top out at $82,500.

So, getting back to this idea of buying a new Jag in the U.S., you're going to need somewhere between $47,000 and $174,000. That means you'll have to be willing to pay two, three, four, five, six or seven times what lots of other people pay for their new cars. Just a passing observation.

In other news, note that if you do buy a new Jaguar in the U.S., you'll be somewhat in the minority. In all of 2012 there were just 12,000 new Jaguars sold here. That compares to 35,000 Porsches, 272,000 Mercedes, 244,000 Lexus, 156,000 Acuras, 149,000 Cadillacs, and 600,000 Ford F-series pickup trucks. Buying a new Jaguar shows that you don't just follow the herd and suggests that you are smarter and more discerning than the average buyer of a premium vehicle. Or, that you are an idiot. It's kind of hard to tell. Either way, you're not completely alone. And Jaguar sales, both in the US and globally, have been rising recently. There were just 50,678 new Jags purchased in the entire world in 2011, but the figure rose to 53,847 in 2012 and jumped to 76,668 in 2013. The US share of the 2013 total was 16,952, up 43% from 2012.

But now what about the idea of a used Jaguar? It seems clear to me that the best and the brightest of Jaguar buyers--and therefore the smartest and most discerning of all car buyers--are the people who buy used Jags. I recognize that this highly selective group includes me and some might say I am maybe blinded by ego in this matter. But my membership in this group is just a coincidence. And I'm not blind, not really. It might be said that new Jaguars are for people who have more money than brains and I recognize that maybe, possibly, conceptually, in some limited cases, on some abstract level, used Jaguars are for people with neither money nor brains, but if we think about that we'll start laughing again. So let's move along.

Used Jaguars can be divided into two classes depending on the age of the car. Jaguars that are twenty-five years old or less are used cars; Jags that are more than twenty-five years old are classic cars. This is true of most cars, actually. The interesting thing in the case of Jaguar is that the periods divide so neatly in terms of ownership of the company. The current used car period includes all the years of Ford and Tata ownership while the classic car period includes all of the various British owned phases of the company, both nationalized and otherwise. So this is the major decision: used or classic? Both groups have some attractions; both groups have major issues.

Used cars in general are fatally flawed precisely because they are so very similar to new cars and yet so clearly not as good. It's almost impossible to avoid comparing a used car to the new version of the same model and in this comparison the used car will always be found wanting. Once in a while a carmaker will stumble and produce a new version that is in some way notably inferior to the old model, but this is rare and usually controversial. Normally, used cars have nothing to particularly recommend them. They have no unique identity, nothing to make them as interesting as the new ones. In terms of styling and interiors they just look tired. "Yes, yes," we say, "That's what was hot four or five years ago, but the world has moved on." In the premium or performance category especially, the used car is generally less powerful and the level of technology is always lower. In the case that we are discussing here, this means when you buy an older Jaguar you're going to get a really clunky sat-nav system, no MP3 player or Bluetooth, a less powerful and/or less efficient engine, a cassette player in the dash, a multi-disk CD player in the trunk, a shift gate that should be taken out and shot, enough miles so that major components are starting to wear out, and, in the case of a convertible, a "boot cover" that would not have been out of place in the middle ages. And, in most cases, no warranty. And oh yeah, also some paint damage and a chipped windshield. Could well need tires and a brake job too. And what about the oxygen sensor? Probably about to fail. All very depressing.

So how about a classic? At first glance classics are really insane. They have all the problems of a used car and every one is even worse due to the greater wear, greater age, and the difficulty of finding replacement parts. And some of them--the best ones--are really expensive. It's well known that a new car's value starts to depreciate as soon as you drive it off the lot. For many cars the decline in value is quite high in the first two or three years. It then levels off a little but the trend is still quite steeply down. Low miles can boost an old car's value and high miles can scare off buyers of relatively new cars, but these effects are relatively minor. This general downward trend continues for a long time, at least twenty-five years, maybe longer. But it doesn't last forever. Somewhere along the line, the dollar value of a car may well start to go back up. There are a couple of reasons for that. First, the car has become more rare. By the time twenty-five years have passed, the great majority of that model year's cars are gone. Many have been wrecked; many others have been junked or abandoned because of breakdowns that the car's low-income owners did not have the means to repair and that in any case would have cost more than the car's value. Given some level of demand, rarity always builds value. But where does this demand come from? Why do people want to buy old cars? One answer is that it is just a matter of love. "I just always wanted one of those," a person might say, when asked about spending $15,000 on a twenty-five year old Oldsmobile. Or maybe it's "I had a used one of these for a while when I was young and I didn't really have the money then to fix it up properly."

Cars are--I will say again--magical items and magic both

transcends time and gives time its meaning. New cars have a special, powerful magic. But a new car is in some ways like a newborn baby. Newborn babies are all just automatically and undeniably adorable. Part of what moves us about them is that they are so simple and unformed and new; they are the rebirth of life, the miraculous renewal of the cycle, of growing up and doing what we do and finally growing old. They remind us what a wonder life is, not just a baby's or a child's life but all of life. When we see a newborn, we can't help but think of old people who have passed. Similarly, if you love new cars, you have to love old cars for the way they remind us of the unity of our existence. Most of the physical items from our past are long gone, but the moments of our lives that we remember aren't gone at all. In some sense all of our times are just one present moment. An old car can reflect those memories back to us and help us be true to who we are. Or at least some people seem to find it so. Also, old cars can be renewed, which is also a kind of magic.

So what I'm saying is what we all already know. There are people out there who are willing to spend good money on really old cars. Some people prefer to spend just a little money to buy an old piece of junk and then spend a lot more money and vast amounts of time restoring it to fine and fancy condition. Some people have enough money to just directly buy the restored one. Some people have so much money that they can build whole collections of old cars. What this all means is that buying a classic Jaguar can get complicated. When and to what degree an older car stops depreciating depends on several factors. It has elements of pure desire but also passes through pragmatism ("Can I possibly to afford to keep this running?") and eventually morphs into questions like "Can I win a national concours award with this car?" or "How well can this car be expected to perform as a financial investment?"

For Jaguar, the perception in the collector marketplace is that cars from the fifties, sixties and early seventies are very desirable while cars from subsequent years have much less value. This has something to do with the styling and appeal of the early cars, but as we learned from our Jaguar brand history lesson, it also means that cars from the original company overseen by William Lyons are seen as more valuable than the cars from any later era. If you're looking to buy an old Jaguar, this is both good news and bad. The bad news is that if you are in sync with the market and you too wish to own a fifties era XK120, a sixties era Mark II or any sort of E-Type; you're going to have to pay through the nose. The good news is that if you want anything else, there are bargains to be had.

Here are some very rough comparisons based on prices I found on the internet in just a couple hours of searching. These are very rough averages, based on the late 2013 asking price for cars in good to excellent condition. "Good to excellent," by the way, does not include concours quality. That's another step up and cars in that category can fetch double or triple the prices below. First, here's a semi-random list of 2013 asking prices for 1964 cars:

1964 Chevrolet Chevelle	$18,000
1964 Mercedes SL	$18,000
1964 Cadillac Eldorado	$20,000
1964 Jaguar Mark II	$28,000
1964 Jaguar E-Type	$75,000
1964 Chevrolet Corvette	$38,000

Now some 2013 asking prices for a selection of 1984 cars:

1984 Cadillac	$5,000-10,000
1984 Chevrolet Caprice	$6,000
1984 Chevrolet Corvette	$8,000
1984 Jaguar XJS	$10,000
1984 Mercedes SL Convertible	$12,000

We can see that indeed the older cars are worth quite a bit more than the newer ones. There is big money interest in the best of the sixties cars, so if you want one you'll have to pony up. You do have the option, I should mention, of turning your attention to lesser cars. Sixties Fiats and Studebakers, for example, are a lot cheaper, even when in concours condition.

So if you're longing for a Studebaker... well, that's fine, but you're reading the wrong book. When we look at the younger cars, we can see, fortunately, that there is little big money interest in mid-eighties cars. This is also true of the nineties for the most part. The good news for Jaguar buyers is that there is a wide range of model years that are relatively affordable. This includes almost all Jaguars made between 1980 and 1991, which I consider to be at least bordering on the classic category, as well as all the cars made between 1992 and roughly 2005, which I am counting as used cars. You will very rarely see asking prices higher than $20,000 and many cars will be available for less than $10,000. Mileage and condition will be more important than specific years.

And what about depreciation? Obviously the 1964 cars stopped depreciating quite some time ago. Their prices have since been rising and that general trend seems likely to continue. For the 1984 cars the picture is not so clear. It seems possible that some or all of them may have 'bottomed out' at this point. The 1984 Corvette, for example, is not depreciating any longer. It's likely that well cared for '84 Corvettes are now actually rising in value. Will the same thing happen to Jaguars, especially the XJS cars from 1980 to 1995, or the XJ and XK8 cars from 1996 to 2005? The answer to that is a resounding maybe.

On the plus side, the XJS is a beautiful, luxurious and powerful car, not to everyone's taste perhaps but still striking. The basic sort of vehicle that it is makes it inherently more collectible than 90% of its automotive brethren. Current taste in car shapes does not favor the straight lines that were common in the XJS era, but popular taste always changes and what is out always comes back in eventually. Another major attraction is the exotic and beautiful Jaguar V-12 engine. On the down side, Jaguar build quality is now felt to have been low during most of the XJS era and many of its complex systems are expensive to repair. Also working against the XJS is the fact that so many of them exist. The XJS was produced from 1975 to 1996, a production life of twenty-one years during which 115,413 cars were made. Still, I find it hard to believe that the

XJS cars from this era will depreciate very much further. Mileage, condition and particular model year preferences will come to matter more and more and almost certainly some prices are already rising.

The situation for 1996 to 2005 cars is that depreciation is still continuing. Jaguars from the early 90's to 2005 are easy to find under $10,000, with many under $5,000. Build quality is considered good, but many of the cars this age are just old enough for lots of things to start going wrong. I personally love their styling, which I find both beautiful and distinctive for its era. But the shapes are not quite as striking or immediately recognizable as those of the E-Type, the Porsche 911, or even the XJS. Ten to fifteen year old cars generally lack glamour. For the Jaguars from this era, the glamour may well return some day, but probably not for a few years yet. If a person were so inclined, a person could buy one of these cars and shut it up in a shed for the next twenty-five years. Then if the person were still alive and the shed were still standing, a person could open it up and try putting the car on the market. That would be fun, but even then I don't think you'd make a fortune. It would be a lot more fun to snap up one of these bargain cars and drive it around.

What about mileage? At what point do the many thousands of miles that a certain car has been driven become too many thousands of miles? Is it at 20,000? 30,000? 50,000? 100,000? When I was looking for my car I ran across an offer on e-Bay for a 2004 XKR with just 17 miles on it, something like that. It was in Maine and the claim was that it had been put into storage immediately upon arrival to our shores. There was no asking price or reserve listed, so I don't know what the owner hoped to get for it. But I'm sure it wasn't cheap. Could it possibly be worth more now than its original price adjusted for inflation? Somehow I don't see that happening, not for a while, maybe not ever. It would certainly be fun to own it, fun to go out and drive around in a ten-year-old brand new car and fun maybe enter it in a show. On the other hand, if the owner were to ask somewhere in the neighborhood of its original price of $85,000, you'd have to be thinking about what else you could get with that money, such as, say, a brand new F-Type, just to name one. If you're interested in this sort of thing, moderation is the key. Most ten year old cars that I've seen with fewer than 5,000 miles are just priced too high. Maybe it pencils out as a long term investment. But spending up to $50,000 for a car that age doesn't appeal to me. If you really care about miles, better to look for the same model with 10,000 to 30,000 miles and priced around twenty or less. Me? I wanted a recent year, so I had to set my mileage limit high. I was willing to go up to 60,000 miles. You worry about a car with that many miles, but prices are reasonable and chances are that not everything is going to fall apart right away.

Another issue in buying your used Jaguar is the question of who to buy from. Of course it is best to buy locally from a private party whose address you know, someone that you can easily have beaten up or murdered if you get ripped off, but that is not always possible. Another safe alternative is your nearest Jaguar dealership, but they are likely to be expensive and the selection of used vehicles may be limited. Because Jaguars are fairly rare, you may have to expand your search area by getting on the internet. You will then find that there are lots of Jaguars available in the southeast, mainly Florida, and the northeast, notably Connecticut. If you are close to either of those places, that's nice for you. If not, you will find that there are a few cars scattered around various other parts of the country as well. You'll have to decide how far you're willing to travel. Personally, living in Oregon, I rejected all Texas cars as being too far away, but I was ready for Salt Lake City or Seattle. The car in Salt Lake was gone before I could make an offer and the one in Seattle seemed a little steep, so I ended up buying from a dealer in California. It was a wonderful experience, wonderful in the same way as jumping out of an airplane and finding that your main parachute was missing and your reserve chute was stuck in its little bag and wouldn't come out without a lot of tugging and clawing at it though it finally did open just in time to make your contact with the ground survivable and you didn't even have to go to the hospital-- which is always good if you think about it.

I bought my car from a guy whose basic business model was consignment sales. Let's call him Joe. What Joe would do is look on Craigslist for people trying to sell higher end cars. He'd call them up--or get his girlfriend to do it--and make the car owner an offer. Give me the car for ninety days, he'd say, and if it doesn't sell I promise to buy it from you myself for an amount that we're going to agree on right here at the beginning. Does this sound too good to be true? Hmm, let's call it borderline. Anyway, the previous owner of my car took him up on it.

I come into the picture when I see the car on the internet. It's what I'm looking for, kind of, a little expensive compared to others around the country but not outrageously so and it's a pretty rare car--the Portfolio Edition in Jupiter red. But I have to think about it and look around a bit more. About three weeks later it's still there and I decide to get serious. I figure I can drive down there and look at it, but I'll give them a call first. So I talk to Joe. What a nice, sincere guy. He says there's no need for me to come down. He'll have his guy drive it up to my place and drive back down in my trade. He offers me an okay trade price. He mentions that the car has a transferable extended warranty good for another eighteen months. He sends electronic copies of the warranty documents. He says that there is some minor but noticeable damage to the left rear wheel and refers me to the photo on his website that shows it clearly. Otherwise, he says, "This car is a 10."

I decide to look at little harder to see if Joe's business is real, and not just a website and a phone number. Turns out it is real, it actually exists at a certain address and also has an extensive Yelp history. For what it's worth, I read it all. I find that Joe has ostensibly made a lot of people happy. *What a nice, sincere guy! He makes everything easy. I'd been trying to sell my Porsche for months; I finally went to Joe and he took care of it. I highly recommend Joe. Joe's great.* But Joe has also apparently pissed some people off. *He sold my car but kept me waiting for my money. I finally got a check, but it bounced. So did the next one. On the third try I finally got paid. I told him I wasn't interested in his offer; then two days later somebody called me again with the same offer. This happened three times. They're totally* *disorganized; there are no files in the office, just a bunch of cardboard boxes full of papers. Joe sold my car but never told me...*etc. Anyway, it's Yelp, so what can you say? My feeling was that at least some of the negatives and at least some of the positives were both real. Joe was running a somewhat sketchy operation with frequent cash flow issues. Still, the operation had been ongoing, at least for a few years. And I figured that as a buyer I was not so much at risk as were the consigners. So I went for it. And was it ever easy, at least at the beginning. We signed some papers over email and the car soon appeared in my driveway, delivered by Joe's young apprentice, another friendly and sincere guy. The car was not a disappointment. It wasn't really a 10, more like a 7.8, but I had assumed that from the start and I was happy to get it.

Of course I didn't have the title. That was still being processed through California DMV. And the extended warranty hadn't been transferred either. That would also take some time. Yes, indeed. They did take time, a long time, and also many calls and emails from me to Joe reminding him that time was passing. Darn it, Joe, I wanted to say, paw through those cardboard boxes, find my paperwork and get this over with! Well, the thing is, Joe eventually did come through. The title transfer came from their DMV to mine and I also got a nice letter from the warranty company saying it was now in my name. I have since made a claim on the warranty and it worked. So my initial judgment of Joe's operation was accurate: shaky but still functional on a basic level. So even now, I have to say, Joe did okay by me.

His operation didn't last though. Turns out he couldn't quite keep it together. Just about five months after my last conversation with him, Joe's business suddenly ceased to exist. The office was vacant; the lot was empty. A tow truck, someone said, had taken away all of the cars, one by one. That meant that Joe--or someone--had basically stolen all the cars that people had consigned to him. In some cases, Joe had delivered cars to buyers, collected the money and never bothered to inform the consigners. In two cases he delivered cars and collected cash from buyers when in fact the cars in question were still owned by the banks that had made loans to the original consigners. Oops. These new customers had the unpleasant experience of buying a car for cash and then having it repossessed a week or so later. After a while Joe was arrested and charged with six counts of grand theft. Presumably the prosecutors chose the six strongest cases out of a total of 30 or more owners who got ripped off.

These events made the local TV news and there is video still out there as I write this. The local reporter is standing on Joe's recently emptied lot recounting the dramatic story. News reports have also revealed Joe's real name, a name that he was definitely not using when I dealt with him. A Google search for that name shows that he was entered into one nationally sanctioned poker tournament, where he won a $600 prize for finishing in tenth place. In his earlier years, he was a partner in a Nissan dealership that went bankrupt owing $850,000 to Nissan and $970,000 in unpaid sales taxes to the State of California. This was not the record for the largest tax cheater in California, but it did put him into the top five. I don't know what has happened since his arrest. The California Department of Corrections has a 'find an inmate' search page and I looked there for him without success, but it might be too soon for that. Or maybe he made bail and skipped. Or maybe he gave back all the cars. I don't know. I kind of liked Joe, as of course all his customers and victims were meant to. I can only be thankful that in my case he was still making an effort to do things right.

So there you have it, as my second wife used to say. Buying a used Jaguar is a messy proposition. Classic era Jaguars from the fifties and sixties are expensive and not real practical. Those from the mid seventies to mid nineties are cheaper but they have their issues. The ones from the Ford era lack charisma as compared to their ancestors. Recent Jaguars from the Tata era are great but generally still so expensive that you can get a really nice new car of some other brand for the same money as the used Jaguar. It's only the 1985 to 2005 Jags that are affordable, and they're falling apart and even when running are hopelessly low-tech. Plus, even if you do find the perfect car for you, it might turn out that the sale involves dealing with someone of dubious moral character. So thank goodness I've shown you the folly of buying a used Jaguar. That alone should make you glad you read this book.

Of course, you being you, you might just go off and buy a used Jaguar anyway. If you did, presumably you'd spend $10-30,000 and put aside another $2,000 or so for repairs or tires or whatever, things that just might pop up in the first year or so. You might not care about Blue Tooth or the J-Gate. You'd put the chipped paint out of your mind. You'd notice that the stereo might be old-fashioned but it still sounded pretty darn good. You'd notice that although the engine didn't have the same 550 hp of the newest ones, it still had enough power to move you along right nicely. You'd notice that you felt good behind the wheel, that the person next to you was comfortable and very likely smiling. You might notice some people noticing you, and maybe they'd be thinking that you had a car that was something special, that had some kind of spark or passion that their cars lacked. You'd notice that on long trips the car just effortlessly ate up the miles. You might think of William Lyons' motto for Jaguar: "Grace, pace and space." The words might even seem appropriate. You might be really happy, at least for a while. It's a little iffy, but you might.

Photo Credits

Red 2005 Porsche Carrera convertible, photographed by Norbert Aepli at the Geneva Motor Show.

Silver Mercedes Benz SL500 photographed in 2004 by Bollar.

Blue-gray Maserati convertible photographed at the Genena Motor Show by Semnoz, March 12, 2004.

Black Jaguar XKR Convertible at the 2008 Sofiero Classic car show in Helsingborg, Sweden. Photo by Magnus Bäck.

Maroon Jaguar SS 100, photographed in 2007 by Jed.

White Jaguar XK 120, photographed in 2009 by Alf Van Beem at the National Oldtimer Festival at Circuit Park Zandvoort in The Netherlands.

Red early 90's Honda NSX, photographed in 2009 by Charles01.

Yellow 90's era Lamborghini Diablo was photographed by Sujit Kumar in 2007.

Understeer diagram by Den Hieperboree at nl.wikipedia.

Understeering open-wheeled car photo by Frank Goldsmith.

Oversteering Mercedes photo by Raimond Spekking.

Panthera onca photo by spacebirdy/CC-BY-SA-3.0 //commons.wikimedia.org/wiki/File:Pantera_onca_-_Tiergarten_Sch%C3%B6nbrunn.jpg

Turning forces diagram by Wersję rastrową wykonał użytkownik polskiego projektu wikipedii: Andrzejmat, Zwektoryzował: Krzysztof Zajączkowski.

All other photos by the author.

About the Author

Michael Witbeck is an educator, auto enthusiast and writer who has lived and worked in a number of exotic locations around the world including Utah, Japan, Spain, Yemen, Cyprus and Turkey. In all these places he has managed to find something to drive. He currently lives in Oregon with a beautiful wife and a lovely dog. Also near at hand is a fine Jaguar automobile, which has recently been reporting both a DSC system fault and a suspension error but which is, nevertheless, a wonderful thing to own.

Other books by this author include a memoir entitled *Auto Biography: A life in the age of the automobile* and an ebook novel called *The Adventures of Rudi the Rational Man*.

Auto Biography begins with the author's first turns behind the wheel of a Case orchard tractor and continues on to the incident with the 1963 Ford Thunderbird and the gas pump, then passes through the Triumph years, the Land Cruiser period in the High Yemen, and the Miata near-decade, with side trips on a Yamaha scooter and in more than one Renault. It contains numerous photographs and is available at GrassRootsBookstore.com.

The *Adventures* tells the story of Rudi the do-nut maker who loses his job but meets a really interesting mute at the unemployment office, which in due course leads to an encounter with the mysterious Rhonda Lingo, then to a difficult sojourn abroad, and finally to rebirth as a muffin baker and holder of a least a part of the secret to everything. It can be downloaded from the iBookstore or from Smashwords.com.

www.ingramcontent.com/pod-product-compliance
Lightning Source LLC
Chambersburg PA
CBHW040732240426
43666CB00043B/1